PENANG

THROUGH GILDED DOORS

JULIA DE BIERRE

PHOTOGRAPHY BY JAMES BAIN SMITH

ARECA
BOOKS

In fond memory
of my parents,
Frederick and Hazel Weatherly

CONTENTS

PREFACE

'Just one more look!' This was my childhood refrain as I broke free from adults' constraints and scrambled over monsoon drains and grassy verges to catch a glimpse of yet another extraordinary building to add to my Penang 'collection.'

Best of all was the indigo-blue mansion in George Town, whose advanced state of decay exerted a special fascination. Peering over blackened walls I would sometimes see children playing badminton amongst a wreckage of abandoned tools. Gilded doors, flung wide open, revealed both grandeur and ruin. The house had a story, but, as with so many of the houses I admired, it remained untold.

Fast-forward to the 21st century and Khoo Su Nin's seminal book 'Streets of George Town' has since retrieved many of the untold stories and changed the way both Penangites and visitors see the island. Meanwhile, my childhood favourite, the Blue Mansion, has been restored to former splendour by its present owners and - serendipity - is now my 'home away from home'.

Honed by a career in the decorative arts, my adult eyes continue to feast on the visual elements of one of Asia's most richly diverse destinations, whilst my heart is warmed by the unique qualities of multi-ethnic Malaysians and their different histories.

Creating this book has been a remarkable journey. It has been shared and greatly enhanced by virtuoso artist and photographer James Bain Smith.

I am equally privileged to have Penang-based Areca Books as my publisher: their active commitment to human, environmental and heritage issues is a source of inspiration. May this book, pleasing to the eye, also make a humble contribution to those essential causes.

Delicately painted gable wall of the Cheah Kongsi in Armenian Street, the heritage heart of George Town. This Kongsi, or clan house, comprising a temple, a small museum, administrative offices and a garden, is just one example of the many newly renovated buildings in the city.

EARLY DAYS

There is something delightfully satisfactory about the shape of Penang Island - 285 square kilometres of sea turtle, basking in the warm waters of the Straits of Melaka, its front flippers formed by the twin promontories of Muka Head and George Town and the dome of its carapace shielded by verdant jungle and forest. And how auspicious - in a region where auspices, both good and bad, can be of prime concern - that Penang's contours should so pleasingly resemble this potent symbol of strength, endurance and longevity.

For many centuries, the island had served as a trading and replenishment post for sea-faring merchants, its safe natural harbour providing necessary shelter during the stormy monsoon months. Plentiful supplies of fresh water and firewood were an added attraction, as was the presence of the areca palm or, to give it its Malay name, the 'pokok pinang'. Tall and slim with feathery leaves, its precious fruit is the betel nut, highly prized not just as a mild stimulant and medical remedy, but also for the important and symbolic role it played, and still plays, in ceremonial offerings and rituals.

By the 16th century, European maritime nations, oblivious to the merits of the betel, were racing to gain a significant toehold in the region for a different reason: the hugely profitable spice trade. Today, it is hard to imagine just how valued the modest pepper, clove and nutmeg were in many parts of the globe, luring explorers, merchants and plunderers to the Malay Archipelago on their route to the principal source of these spices: the Moluccan Islands.

Above: Betel nut from the 'pokok pinang', the palm from which the island takes its name.
Left: The Waterfall has a great historic, symbolic and practical significance for the inhabitants of Penang.

In 1511, when the region's foremost trading entrepôt, the great Islamic Sultanate of Melaka, situated just south of Penang, fell to the Portuguese, it was hardly surprising that other foreign powers, greedy for their slice of the lucrative spice cake, began sharpening their knives in earnest. It was the end of an era and for the local people a golden age of history was coming to a close.

The Dutch East India Company was the next to impose its presence in the Malay Archipelago, capturing Melaka from the Portuguese in 1641. By now, other trade routes had been opened up, other far-flung lands seized and colonised, and other essential and inessential luxuries had become all the rage in chilly northern lands. Increasing competition meant that trading companies had to be much more structured and the Dutch East India Company, with its tentacular grip on world markets, its creation of monopolies and its high yielding share certificates, was the Big White Chief of them all.

The British East India Company, established in 1600, was also actively expanding the frontiers of trade and Empire. However, Bengal headquarters turned a deaf ear when, in 1771, a thirty-one year old trader with a pioneering spirit tried to interest the Company in establishing a military and mercantile base on a small tropical island he had recently visited on the other side of the Indian Ocean.

A base, he insisted, that would not only provide a strategic bastion against the Dutch and the French but was also in a prime position for the burgeoning trade between India and China. Ships could be constructed and repaired there, warehouse facilities erected, and myriad possibilities envisioned for attracting the labour needed to build the infrastructure of a great mercantile centre. There was even land suitable for plantations.

The visionary young man went by the name of Captain Francis Light and the island, of course, was Penang.

Inhabited by Malay fishing, agricultural and trading communities, the island appears in the navigational drawings of the celebrated Admiral Cheng Ho as early as the 15th century.

FRANCIS LIGHT

Above: *Fort Cornwallis, built on Light's initial landing point, is considered a landmark monument in Malaysia's historical development. In 2001, a major restoration was completed, spearheaded by the Department of Museums and Antiquity. Objects discovered during excavations included coins and tobacco pipes but no weapons.*

Top right: *Francis Light statue, outside the Penang State Museum.*

Bottom right: *Francis Light is buried in the Christian Cemetery, along with fellow settler James Scott and David Brown of Glugor Estate.*

The story of Francis Light is so inextricably linked to Penang's dense narrative and has been recounted so often that it is tempting to follow the well-trodden path of the classic annals: to wit, the birth of Light in the County of Suffolk, England in 1740, his grammar school education, his brief enrolment in the Navy and his subsequent embarkation for India on a merchant vessel belonging to the East India Company.

In Madras, he secured command of a ship belonging to the trading company, Jourdain, Sullivan and De Souza, and set sail for Kedah, situated on the north-west side of the Malay Peninsula.

He lost no time, it appears, in learning the Malay language, cultivating good relations with the Sultan of Kedah and familiarising himself with the region. This included Penang, which at that time was under the control of Kedah.

Anxious to break free from Siam's (Thailand) claims of suzerainty and hoping for protection from the fierce coastal assaults of marauding pirates, the Sultan was persuaded by Light that by leasing Penang to the East India Company, he would receive both military assistance and financial benefits. However, as we know, when Light relayed the good news back to head office, there was little enthusiasm for his scheme.

Disappointed, the trader continued his seafaring activities in the region, basing himself in Junk Ceylon (Phuket) with his common-law wife of Eurasian descent, Martina Rozells. Finally, fifteen years after his initial proposal, the East India Company encouraged Light to resume negotiations with the new Sultan.

Mission accomplished, Light landed on the island in 1786 with a motley retinue of soldiers and bearers and proudly raised the British flag on the spit of land that would become Fort Cornwallis.

Fortunately for posterity, the pallid new name chosen for the settlement 'The Prince of Wales Island' was never more than a damp squib; the real fireworks came from the Sultan of Kedah, who, finding that the British promises of protection were unforthcoming, had to resort to gunboat diplomacy in order to seal the deal.

Once the occupation was legalised, Penang became part of British India and Light, as first Superintendent of the island, found himself treading a thorny path: on one side lay his responsibilities to an Empire ridden with ingrained racial prejudice and a rigid class system, whilst on the other side lay his personal life, an assimilation of local customs and an attachment to Asia and its diverse peoples.

Official records, sadly, give us little intimate knowledge of this fascinating adventurer, anymore than his imposing bronze statue cast, for want of an available likeness, in the effigy of his son William, can give us any real idea of what he looked like. Exhausted by his largely understaffed efforts and stricken, apparently, with malaria, he died in Penang in 1794, just 8 years after his arrival.

Was he the man the memorial plaque, placed in the Grecian rotunda just outside Penang's Anglican Church, would have us believe? 'The Settlers and Natives were greatly attached to him and by his death had to deplore the loss of one who watched over their interests and cares as a Father' runs the legend.

Or was he an energetic opportunist, a profiteering buccaneer, destined to be embalmed by colonial textbook history in a conveniently thick coat of respectability? And what of his intriguing companion, Martina Rozells, whose mixed origins remain so mysterious, but could in part be traced back to an eponymous French family attached to Louis XIV's Embassy in Siam?

Whatever the truth - or truths - about their personal history, of one thing we can be certain, as we commence our exploration of George Town: namely, the important and far-reaching role Captain Francis Light played in the city's initial conception and eventual evolution.

Early European travellers to Penang were fascinated by Mother Nature's scale and diversity - the luxuriance of the vegetation, the strangeness of the fruits, the oddity of the animals. Expeditions were invariably made to visit two essential tourist sights (or 'lions' as they were quaintly called) - the first was to the torrential cascades of the Waterfall and the second was to the Great Tree.

A number of 19th century paintings and drawings attest to the extraordinary dimensions of this legendary tree, although its exact botanical species has remained elusive. Today, Penang is still graced with great trees.

GEORGE TOWN

George Town? In the disarming way that nothing here is necessarily quite as it seems, George Town is actually a city (since 1957), an extraordinary city, a city for adventurers and explorers, for seafarers and merchants, for strugglers and romantics, a city where the rich and the poor, the skilled and the unskilled, continue to live and work side-by-side just as they have done for more than two centuries, in a relatively unchanged environment.

How, the visitor wonders, has George Town's historic inner city - an urban time-capsule boasting the most outstanding and comprehensive collection of 19th and early 20th century buildings in South-East Asia - managed to escape the relentless march of 'progress'?

The Rent Control Act, instigated in 1948 and only repealed in 2000, was certainly one of the major reasons. Low rents meant that the small-earners - the artisans, hawkers, astrologers et al - could afford to live and ply their trade within the city. Low rents also meant that landlords were less inclined to modernise or demolish: the returns were too meagre. Entire swathes of the city remained untouched, preserved in a lively decay recalling Venice, New Orleans or Havana.

It is still too early to see how radically the repeal will affect this unique urban heritage or, more importantly, the life of its inhabitants. Enlightened Penangites strive - with heartening success - to conserve and restore the city, whilst maintaining traditional neighbourhoods and precious, multi-ethnic community life.

For the fabulous story of George Town is, above all, about its people. It is they, with their culture, traditions, festivals and just plain work-a-day life that give breadth and vitality to the city's remarkable streets and buildings.

On a clear day you can see… Bukit Mertajam, for centuries a vital landmark for seafarers. As viewed from Penang Road, George Town's main artery, looking over the undulating roofs of the Elite shophouses in Muntri Street. Many of these houses have at least two inner courtyards.

THE INFANT COLONY

The swampy promontory where Captain Light landed and intended to build his settlement already had a name: *Tanjung Penaga* or Penaigre Point, an appellation it took from the wild forests of Penaga Laut - a beautiful tropical tree with creamy white flowers - that grew right down to the shore. And as Light's men started to clear the land, they were met with a silent, sylvan army of resistance: the trees proved impossible to fell. Tools buckled against the hard wood, axes broke, hatchets split, tempers boiled under the burning sun.

Local legend has it that, at this point, Light loaded a cannon with Spanish dollars, fired it into the enemy forest and let human nature take its course: within no time, it seems, his comrades' motivation to find the silver coins was such that the forest was quickly cut down and defeated. Urbanization could now march ahead.

Light's early plans for 'George Town' as it was now called, in honour of Britain's King George III, seem, with hindsight, surprisingly *ad hoc* and elementary. The choice of a low-lying site, subject to floods, the absence of an effective fresh water supply close by and the lack of spatial structure are all evidence that, as far as the East India Company was concerned, the main purpose of Penang was as a 'get rich quick' trading post and a useful but fleeting port of call. Hatching the embryo of a future great metropolis was certainly not high on the East India Company agenda.

Whatever Light's shortcomings as a town planner, the simple grid of streets that he laid out and named remains to this day. Light Street, Beach Street (which at that time ran along the shore), Chulia Street and Pitt Street (now Jalan Masjid Kapitan Keling): four streets to embrace the inner city nucleus and contain the increasingly diverse ethnic groups that were flooding into George Town, from near and far, to participate in Light's ambitious dream.

Right: The Convent at Light Street, founded by French nuns. In 1859 it took up premises in what was the original Government House. It is the oldest girls' school in Malaysia.
Above: *Within Convent Walls: a view from one of the earliest public buildings in Penang.*

Right: St. George's Church, the earliest Anglican church in South-East Asia. (see text overleaf) In the foreground stands the rotunda, dedicated to Captain Francis Light.

Above: A much later monument, the Queen Victoria Diamond Jubilee Clocktower, 60 feet high, one foot for each year of her reign. A gift from a Chinese businessman, it was only completed in 1902, by which time Victoria's son Edward was firmly on the throne...

A vision of early Penang is inevitably shaped and coloured by the pictorial evidence of the time - oil paintings, watercolours and engravings. Since much of this artistry was accomplished by the British, for the British, a layperson might be forgiven for thinking that Penang in the 1800's was largely composed of elegantly attired 'ladies and gentlemen' disporting themselves in an idealised setting sometimes more redolent of Scotland than the tropics.

The reality is that the first British settlers amounted to a tiny minority, a couple of hundred heads at most. Existing local communities were now joined by fellow Malays, Indians, Chinese, Burmese, Arabs and Eurasians, to name just a few of the early pioneers. Although there was no formal segregation between the different races, Francis Light assigned a street in George Town to each community; the Europeans clustered together in makeshift bungalows around the north beach area of Light Street where the proximity of the public well was no doubt considered an advantage. Unfortunately, the well-water was stained distressingly red - a belated revenge, no doubt, from the still intact roots of the Penaga Laut.

The fundamentally commercial aspirations of the settlement were reflected in the early developments, which were of a pragmatic nature: modest dwellings, warehouses, offices, jetties, a garrison, a prison, a hospital, and, perhaps most tellingly, a Christian cemetery.

It is here, in this gentle shady place, that the notion that Penang was once part of British India becomes a tangible reality. Not just because the plethora of marble cupolas, obelisks and urns conjures up the decayed grandeur of the *Raj*, but also because the sepulchral inscriptions remind us that many of the deceased were originally sent to Penang from the Indian subcontinent in order to escape - or recover from - the rampant diseases and debilitating climate that decimated these pale-faced *ferringhi*. Sad irony, as it appears that they fared no better in Penang than in Madras, Bombay or Calcutta.

Penang was linked to India not just through British officialdom but also through the Indian soldiers, merchants and manual workers it brought in its wake. By the early 19th century convict labour, principally from Bengal, was being used to build roads, bridges, an aqueduct and a viable path up Penang Hill. Convicts - some of whom were, in fact, political dissenters - were also used to build the first public edifices.

Unsurprisingly, many of the colonial buildings resembled their counterparts on the Indian subcontinent and, similarly, demonstrated the manner in which a classical language of architecture could be ingeniously adapted to suit local conditions and climate. One of the most noteworthy examples is St. George's Church, whose cool Ionic beauty was offset by louvred shutters and glassless apertures allowing for a free flow of air, glimpses of exotic vegetation, and the sound of tropical bird song as sweetly melodious as that of any choir. Completed in 1818 by Captain Robert Smith of the Bengal Engineers (the same Smith who painted skilful early views of Penang), the church was inspired by St. George's Cathedral in Madras, which in turn was modelled on James Gibb's 1726 masterpiece, the London church of St. Martin-in-the-Fields. (Pattern books such as Gibb's 1728 'Book of Architecture' were an invaluable source for that unsung hero of colonial architecture, the British military engineer, and the popularity of these books can also explain why building styles in the colonies sometimes appear a century or so after their inception in Europe.)

But the jewel in the crown of Penang's early pioneer past is undoubtedly the recently restored Suffolk House, Francis Light's country estate. From modest beginnings it evolved, in the early 19th century, into a magnificent example of the Anglo-Indian 'Garden House' - a verandahed Georgian palace, complete with ballroom, in an Arcadian setting.

After the 1857 Indian Mutiny, the debt-ridden East India Company lost its administrative powers and was eventually dissolved; barely a decade later, in 1867, Penang, now part of the Straits Settlements along with Malacca and Singapore, became a Crown Colony. These administrative changes were reflected in the municipal architecture: since Britain's interests were ostensibly no longer merely mercantile, a sense of Pomp, Circumstance and Empire became the order of the day.

And, as George Town flourished and grew, the European community moved into leafy residential suburbs, and around this enclave sprung up botanical gardens, sports fields, a Masonic lodge and exclusive clubs.

Pimms, anyone?

Above: The State Assembly, Light Street. Built in the early 19th century, it originally served as Magistrates' Courts. Typical of the high Palladian style of many Anglo-Indian public buildings, with a grand portico and classical columns, ideally suited to the climate and light.
Bottom Left: The recently renovated Town Hall, built circa 1880.
Far left: Windows in charming Gothick style.
Top left: Suffolk House. 'I give and bequeath…unto. Martina Rozells, the pepper Gardens with my Garden house plantations and all the Land by me cleared in that part of the Island called Suffolk.'
Francis Light's will, 1794.

ENCLAVES: *The Hidden City*

Colonial enclaves, clan enclaves, commercial enclaves, religious enclaves... multi-ethnic George Town forms a complex patchwork of neighbourhoods, with invisible parameters and overlapping boundaries, stitched together by strong threads of tolerance and understanding. It was inevitable, given the early pioneers' fascinatingly diverse origins, that they should create no ordinary city but instead an urban treasury of remarkable buildings, miniature 'cities within the city' which, miraculously, still survive today.

ACHEEN STREET

One of the oldest enclaves can be found in Acheen Street and has as its focus the *Mesjid Melayu*, or the Acheen Street Mosque. Built in 1808, at the behest of a spice-trading Acehnese prince of Arab descent, Tengku Syed Hussain, the mosque features an octagonal minaret from which, five times a day, the haunting call to prayer resonates across the neighbourhood. The wealthy Tengku, accompanied by his extended family, had settled in Penang in 1792, after negotiating recognition of Islamic law with Francis Light. Soon, fellow traders from all parts of the Malay Archipelago and even the Arab world followed his example.

As the 19th century progressed, the initial *kampung* became a flourishing and entrepreneurial Muslim community, which lived, worked, and prayed together. Pepper traders, diamond merchants and shipbrokers fraternised with booksellers, religious scholars, teachers and intellectuals. Up until the 1970's, Penang was one of the leading ports in the region for the chartered pilgrim ships taking Muslims to Mecca to perform the spiritual journey of the *haj*; naturally, the leading 'pilgrim-brokers' were based in Acheen Street. Thousands of pilgrims and family well-wishers, from mainland Malaya, Indonesia and southern Thailand, would converge on this part of town - the 'second Jeddah' - for a few days preceding their departure: the pilgrims to organise their travel logistics and to prepare themselves spiritually at the mosque, the well-wishers to indulge in the marvellous street life and bazaar atmosphere. Air travel brought an end to this convivial pilgrim 'industry' and today Acheen Street is a quieter place.

Left: The Acheen Street Mosque, with its unusual octagonal minaret, is one of Penang's oldest existing mosques. A similar mosque could be found in Aceh, the region that local Moslems looked to as a centre of religious knowledge.

Above: Nearby, the mansion of Acehnese pepper trader Syed Al-Attas has been restored with technical assistance from the French State and houses the Penang Islamic Museum.

Top left: Cikgu Mohamed Yahaya, retired teacher, resides in one of the half-brick, half-wooden houses standing in the waqf (endowed) compound of the Acheen Street Mosque. A descendant of Sheikh Omar Basheer, the celebrated 19th century imam, Sufi mystic and reformist (in particular, the Sheikh campaigned against the stranglehold of the secret societies, rife in the area) Cikgu Mohamed was born in this kampung, like his family before him. He remembers how these houses formed the epicentre of the extraordinary community dynamic generated by the mosque and its spiritual and intellectual life.

He remembers, too, the bustle of the pilgrim trade and the noise of the nearby printing presses. Malay or Arabic-language newspapers, novels and pamphlets, hot off the press, were exported from here or sold in the surrounding bookshops.

Bottom left: Pilgrim tickets to Jeddah, intricate embroidery samples, early Hari Raya greeting cards, Cikgu Mohamed's house is a repository of local memory and culture.

Right: The delightful house, its timber walls painted a cool green, is designed to allow maximum airflow through its open windows and fretwork partitions.

KHOO KONGSI : *a Clan Citadel*

Long before Western incursions into the Malay Archipelago, traders and merchants from the coastal provinces of China had journeyed to the *Nanyang* - traditional Chinese parlance for the 'Southern Seas' - in search of exotic marine and forest produce. Arriving from China laden with silks, porcelain and fragrant teas they returned with a heist of scented woods, birds' nests and a rare gum known as 'dragon's blood'.

By the 15th century, some of these early traders had established second homes in Malacca and Sumatra, taken local, non-Muslim wives and absorbed or subtly modified certain aspects of Malay culture, notably language, dress and cuisine, whilst retaining ancestral Chinese traditions. Their descendants, who became known as *Peranakan* (in Malay: locally born) or, more familiarly *Baba* (for males) and *Nyonya* (for females), also settled in Penang where their numbers were bolstered by the Chinese immigrant influx of the 19th century. Structured clan communities formed, drawn together by common ancestry or dialect ties.

On this *terra incognita* clan affiliation, already an important component of Chinese culture, took on a new dimension: for the *sinkeh* (literally: new guest) belonging to a clan ensured not just protection and support but also served as a potent reminder of ancestral roots and traditions. Clan members built clan houses or *kongsi*; soon these increasingly elaborate edifices, containing temples, meeting places, administrative offices and even accommodation, became an integral part of George Town's social and architectural fabric.

Just off the lower end of Beach Street you will find, hidden down narrow passageways or secluded within tranquil courtyards, the *kongsis* of the 'Hokkien Big Five' - the Cheahs, Lims, Khoos, Tans and Yeohs. Although within easy distance of each other and sharing a clearly defined spatial perimeter, each of these *kongsis* has its own story and aesthetic. Grandest and most lavish of them all is the Leong San Tong Khoo *Kongsi*.

***Above and left**: Clan temple of the Khoo Kongsi, Cannon Square. The layout bears traces of its original construction, an Anglo-Malay bungalow that underwent conversion. In structure and decoration the temple is typical of the South Chinese Fujian style.(Hokkien) Spectacular roofs bear 4 distinct types of decoration: porcelain shardwork, stucco sculpture, ceramic figurines and jiao zhi glazed pottery.*

Above: The Khoo Kongsi evolved against a background of gang warfare, secret societies and inadequate public security; this narrow archway entrance on Beach Street reflects the labyrinthine configuration of a defensive stronghold.
Right: Ancestral hall of the temple. Ancestor worship is a key religious belief for the Chinese: here, gilded wooden tablets inscribed with the name and birth date of the dear departed are arranged in orderly rows on an elaborately carved teak table.

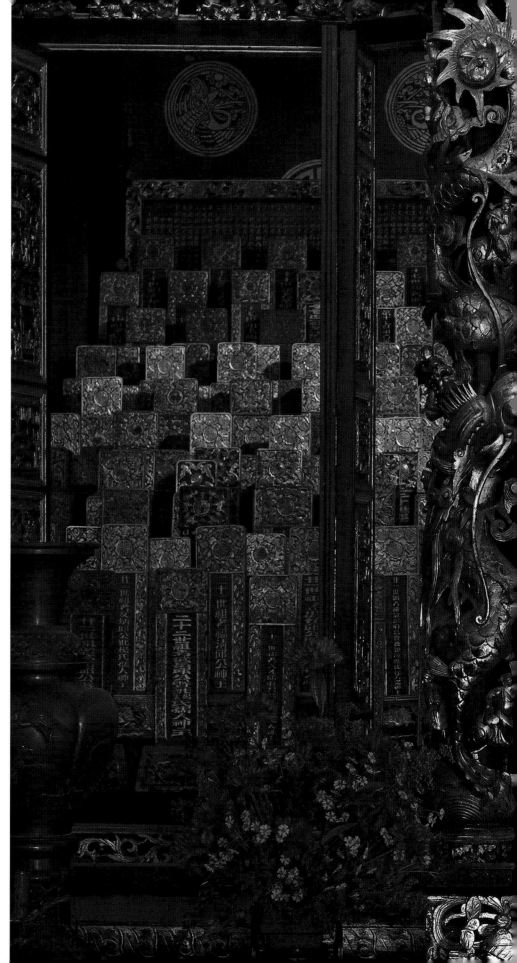

Right: The wealth of decorative detail within the Khoo Kongsi includes stonework, woodcarving, gilding, lacquer-work, murals and calligraphy.
Clockwise: *Figure sculptured in stone, one of a pair, beckoning towards good fortune. A carved and gilded screen in the theatre building. An antique European chandelier in the ancestral hall. A gilded air vent. Window detail featuring carved stone 'bamboo' balustrades. Part of a mural: one of 36 celestial guardians, the work of distinguished artist and man of letters, Yeoh Boon Ngah the Hermit.*
Centre: *the traditional Sikh guard.*

Records tell us that members of the Khoo clan were present in Penang soon after the arrival of Francis Light. Enterprising traders and prosperous businessmen, their numbers increased considerably during the 19th century with the arrival of *sinkeh* from the ancestral village of Sin Kang, in the Sam Toh District, Hai Teng County, Chiang Chew Prefecture, Hokkien Province, China. It is safe to say that this purely geographical incantation would have guaranteed a warm welcome!

In 1850, a British trader sold clan members a plot of land, adjacent to Armenian Street, and they created an extraordinary building complex of a scale and ambition unique in South-East Asia. What began as the far-off echo of a traditional Chinese clan village, with a clan temple - converted from the British trader's Anglo-Malay bungalow - buried within a defensive maze of clan dwellings (each dwelling bearing a black and gold door plaque inscribed '*Sin Kang*' after the ancestral village of the inhabitant), became the veritable citadel we see today.

However often one visits the Khoo *Kongsi*, and whichever of the three elusive entrances one approaches it by, there is always a sense of surprise and wonderment to see the richly ornate and colourful temple, rebuilt in 1906 and splendidly restored in 2001, rising from the austere grey granite of Cannon Square. Just as thrilling is the fact that its historical setting is pedestrian-friendly and totally intact. Within the square stands an outdoor theatre for Chinese opera, administration buildings in Anglo-Indian style and surrounding this inner nucleus a protective 'rampart' of more than 60 traditional row houses of differing epochs.

The *Kongsi* dwelling houses, originally for the sole use of Khoo clan members, now have a more diverse selection of inhabitants and uses and the '*Sin Kang*' door plaque is less in evidence.

Enter the main temple building and prepare to be overawed by a dazzling manifestation of ancestor and deity worship. The central hall, dedicated to two great warriors of Chinese history, patron saints of the clan, is flanked by two halls, one for the altar of *Tua Pek Kong*, the God of Prosperity, and the other for an important display of ancestral tablets. The walls are lined with plaques inscribed with the names of Khoos who have distinguished themselves through public service or academically. And it is here that one realises, looking at the seats of learning mentioned - Oxford, Cambridge *et al* - that the Penang *Baba*, by the 20th century, had acquired yet another layer of culture: that of the British Empire.

KING STREET

A quite different aspect of the enduring legacy of the *kongsi* tradition can be seen in King Street, 'the *kongsi* enclave', where no fewer than twelve Chinese association houses and temples make up one of the most colourful and interesting streets in George Town. In contrast to the *kongsi* enclaves of lower Beach Street, which were conceived as free-standing, independent units set within a courtyard, the temples and association houses here are integrated into, or are extensions of, the surrounding architecture. Temple-townhouses, taller, wider and more ornate versions of the neighbouring residential and commercial buildings, are juxtaposed with classic, single-storey temples to create an architectural ensemble unique in South-East Asia.

As one of the earliest of the principal streets, King Street was also a home for Indian Muslim sailors and dock-workers. Today, the presence of Indian businesses and general street life demonstrates the fluidity of George Town's multi-ethnic communities.

Above: Two outstanding examples of temple-townhouses, housed in association buildings on King Street. The impressive Poe Choo Seah (left), three storeys high, was completed in 1903 and is still in fine condition. The Lee Sih Chong Soo (right) was founded in the 1920's. Note the temple façade grafted onto what is essentially a townhouse.
Opposite: Altar detail at the Poe Choo Seah.

THE CARETAKER

Like his father before him, Mr. Khoo has devoted his life to the maintenance of one of King Street's most impressive association houses, the Poe Choo Seah. The immaculate condition of the interior, with its polished floors, pristine furnishings and perfectly timed clock, testify to his commitment and love for a building that has played, and still plays, an important role in the lives of a choice section of the Straits-born Chinese community.

The spacious, high-ceilinged house is built in the traditional Straits Chinese manner with a granite-lined inner courtyard and a steep wooden staircase enclosed within painted balustrades. It serves not only as a fitting venue for important committee meetings but also contains an upper-floor temple repository for the ancestral tablets of the association members. Carvings and gildings in the temple are of the very finest quality. Established in the 19th century, the association was revived in 1893 under the chairmanship of Cheah Chen Eok, the prosperous Chinese businessman who is best remembered in George Town for his handsome gift of the Queen Victoria Diamond Jubilee Clocktower (see page 22).

Wooden pillars supporting the houses, sturdy enough to withstand fierce tropical storms and strong waves, have to be replaced every few years. The trunk of the nibong palm, available from the nearby mangrove swamps, was the favoured material; concrete columns are a modern alternative.

Dragon boat racing, involving long, specially designed boats, was a colourful and symbolic tradition the clan jetty settlers brought with them from China - today it has evolved into a major Penang festival and sporting event, attracting thousands of international participants.

THE CLAN JETTIES : *A floating population*

Just a few minutes walk from the prestigious banks and offices of Beach Street and the imposing waterfront buildings of Weld Quay lies an infinitely more modest, yet no less precious, link to George Town's shipping and trading history: the clan Jetties. Astonishing water villages built on wooden stilts, they fan out to sea from the busy shoreline in a series of self-contained piers upon which long rows of timber dwellings are connected by planked walkways.

Each jetty bears the name of a Chinese family clan - Chew, Lim, Yeoh, Tan, Lee - and, until recently, the right to reside on a clan name jetty implied ties of kinship to that particular clan. The oldest residential jetty, the Chew Jetty, dates back to the 19th century when single male immigrants named Chew came from China's Southern Fujian province to seek work in Penang's thriving free-trade port. Other immigrants followed, with different names but also from Fujian, and jetties were added and extended as these closely-knit communities of port-workers moored their boats and made their homes just a convenient stone's throw from their livelihood.

Stevedores, lightermen, cargo-handlers, sampan rowers, charcoal-sellers - without this resilient and economical labour force the entrepôt trade would have soon run adrift. Many of these men came to Penang intending to return to China after a few years, with their hard-earned savings; instead, swayed by the certainty of regular work, they stayed, were joined by other kinsmen, married and put down roots. Their wives, in turn, found employment with the ships - preparing meals, doing laundry, and washing the decks.

The marine dwellings became more domesticated: from basic communal shelters they evolved into the compact houses we see today, with fenced-in 'verandah' areas, potted plants to give the illusion of 'terra-firma' and indications of some, if not all, modern comforts.

However, since the demise of Penang's free-port status in 1969, much of this maritime community has gradually had to find alternative work or even move away. On some of the jetties the clan connection has become tenuous, and one or two of them have disappeared to make way for development. Those that remain are a moving testament to the workers whose toils contributed so much to the port's success.

A STREET CALLED HARMONY

More than 100 religious and spiritual sites reflect the ethnic diversity of George Town, where Islamic, Buddhist, Taoist, Confucian, Hindu, Sikh and Christian communities have lived together for more than two centuries. Although Islam is Malaysia's official religion, freedom of worship is guaranteed by the federal constitution.
Above: *Devotee of the Goddess of Mercy Temple. Piles of joss smoulder in the background.*

For living, breathing proof of the continued vibrancy of the world's great religions, there is no better place to look than Jalan Masjid Kapitan Keling - otherwise known as the 'Street of Harmony'. Start at the top end, say, on a Sunday, you will see Anglican worshippers stepping out of St. George's Church, hymn sheets in hand. Continue down the street, any day of the week, and the smoke from burning joss will tell you that you are close to the Goddess of Mercy Temple, the oldest and possibly liveliest Chinese Temple in Penang. Next comes the *Mahamariamman* Temple, dedicated to the Hindu goddess *Mariamman*. By the time you reach the Kapitan Keling Mosque, it is Friday, holy day for Islam, and a steady stream of believers will be making their way to afternoon prayer.

The proximity of these houses of worship is, of course, no coincidence. When Francis Light and his successors drew up the initial plan for George Town, provisions were made so that each ethnic community could establish an appropriate religious edifice. Plots of land were designated for the purpose and this area, then known as Pitt Street after British Prime Minister, William Pitt the Younger, became the favoured spot.

In the close vicinity, other communities also built temples, mosques, shrines and churches. For so many people, Penang represented a safe and liberal haven. Already, in 1786, a group of Roman Catholic Eurasians, victims of religious persecution in Siam and Dutch-controlled Malacca, had arrived in Penang via Kedah, at Francis Light's invitation. Accompanied by Bishop Garnault they settled around what would become Bishop Street and built a wooden church in Church Street.

Everywhere you look, you will see the signs and symbols of the city dwellers' spiritual life. Some signs are almost invisible - glance down and you will see a tiny offering on the pavement, a few crushed petals or a single orange. Stare skywards and you will see minarets, steeples, *gopuram* and curved temple gables. Look straight ahead and you will glimpse a Muslim shrine, erected in memory of a 13th century saint.

No, there is not just one Street of Harmony in George Town, but many.

THE GODDESS OF MERCY TEMPLE

The foundation stone of this popular Chinese Temple, situated in the heart of George Town, was laid in the early 1800's by the pioneer Cantonese and Hokkien immigrants from South China. The temple was apparently dedicated to *Ma Chor Po*, the patron saint of seafarers, in grateful recognition of their safe delivery from the dangers of the South China Sea. As time went by, and the 'seafarers' became urbanised 'islanders', *Kuan Yin*, the Goddess of Mercy, was established as the primary deity.

One of the most beloved deities in the Buddhist tradition, *Kuan Yin* is actually a *Boddhisattva*, the personification of compassion and selflessness, who, despite having discovered Nirvana, remains in this world to guide fellow beings out of suffering and towards the path of enlightenment.

From the beginning, the temple was more than a place of worship; it also served as a town council and tribunal for the Hokkien and Cantonese communities who formed, and still form, the principal Chinese dialect groups of Penang. However, as the 19th century progressed, the rivalry between these groups became such that, eventually, the spiritual and secular were separated and in 1880 a Chinese Town Hall was built next door.

Today, the *Kuan Yin* Temple attracts people from all walks of life. Go to the temple on a feast day and you will be swept up into a maelstrom of smoke, heat, incense, and jostling humanity. The steady tolling of a bell, the fervent faces of the worshippers and the dim, shadowy surroundings combine to make this a mesmerising experience.

Outside, on the granite-paved forecourt, the pageant continues. More smoke, more joss, more devotees. Two huge red burners tower over the crowds, ready to receive the paper wads of hell-money, cash-comfort for the departed. The orange robe of a passing monk glows in the midday sun. A child holding a birdcage opens the wicker door and watches in wonder as the bird flies out and soars to freedom.

Right: Feast day at the Goddess of Mercy Temple, Jalan Masjid Kapitan Keling. A Western-style chandelier and Chinese lanterns illuminate the rapt faces of the worshippers.
Above: Dragon roof guardians, in silhouette against a dramatic sky. A Buddhist monk offers prayers for the devotees.

THE YEOH KONGSI

By the middle of the 19th century, the Chinese community of Penang, composed of different dialect groups, had started to polarise. The Goddess of Mercy Temple, while still the main religious focal point for many people, no longer played quite the federating role of the early days.

Increasingly, clan associations and *kongsi* began collecting funds from fellow members in order to build their own, private clan temples.

Leading this movement were the Hokkien 'Big Five', who, as we have seen, created their own *kongsi* enclave. Among these figure the Yeoh *Kongsi*, founded in 1841. Smaller and less opulent than the nearby Khoo *Kongsi*, it has, nevertheless, a particular charm and atmosphere. Originally, the two-storey building stood near the waterfront and had its own clan jetty; from the upper floor prayer hall clansmen could gaze out to sea. This, of course, would have been in line with the *feng shui* principles of 'viewing-the-sea-from-a-hillside-perch' position.

However, when the seafront was reclaimed and built upon the Yeoh *Kongsi* found itself further inland, with a changed view. Hopefully, other *feng shui* principles now came into play...

The interior of the *kongsi* presents a colourful showcase of traditional Chinese architecture and decorative elements. Gilt and lacquer pillars, ornate wall plaques and huge ceremonial lanterns are offset by the simple modesty of terracotta-tiled floors and pastel coloured walls.

Climb the stairs and you will find the 'Hall of the Four Knows': thus called because of the virtuous Yeoh Mandarin clansman who, when asked to accept a bribe, replied: 'If I accept a bribe, Heaven knows, the Earth knows, I know and you know'.

To this day, integrity and virtue are the rallying call of the Yeohs.

Kongsi houses such as these are still an essential part of community life and, for the younger generation, they serve as a fascinating reminder of where their ancestors came from and the tremendous feats achieved to gain a place in the Penang sun.

Above: In the Yeoh Kongsi, *as in most Chinese temples, the roof structure and decoration is as important inside as it is outside. A truss system of cantilevered units, strengthened by brackets, form an intricate, interlocking puzzle resting on precisely aligned pillars that spread the weight of the heavy terracotta roofing tiles.*

Exposed structural elements allow air to circulate freely. Gilded, carved or painted they become an integral part of the decoration.

Red is a favoured colour in temples, symbolizing the positive Yang principle and encouraging good fortune.

Left: *Interior of the Yeoh Kongsi.*

THE HAN JIANG ANCESTRAL TEMPLE

In 1800, the British, now firmly established on Penang Island, acquired from Kedah a further strip of land just across the sea channel, which they named Province Wellesley, after the Marquis of Wellesley. The new land gave Penang control over its harbour; it also provided useful terrain for plantations. Many of the agricultural workers belonged to the Teochew dialect group - today they form an influential trading community.

The Han Jiang Ancestral Temple of the Penang Teochew Association in Chulia Street was built in 1870. Recently restored, it can be considered one of the most beautiful examples of Teochew temple architecture in South-East Asia. Stepping from the busy commercial street through the unassuming entranceway one is immediately encompassed by another world - a traditional Chinese temple, extending, as is usual, horizontally rather than vertically, with a tranquil walled courtyard, serried ranks of tall lacquered doors and exquisite bas-relief on lime washed walls. The roof, sloping less than its Hokkien counterpart, bears tiny three-dimensional human figures in porcelain shardwork, resembling characters from the celebrated Teochew opera repertoire.

LIONS AND DRAGONS

In most Chinese temples, the roof is the dominant architectural feature: horizontal or curved, its ridge laden with a fantastical bestiary, it gives added shape and panache to a building which, surface embellishments aside, is often a plain square or rectangle.

There is a poetic symbolism, closely connected to nature, attached to the colours, use of materials and architectural construction of temple roofs. The upward sweep of the swallow's tail, the undulating movement of ocean waves and the sinuosity of a crawling cat are all popular images which have been given material form on the temple roof and, since it is commonly believed that demons and evil spirits can only travel in straight lines, designs also try to incorporate curves, broken lines and articulated surfaces.

The intricate cornucopia of roof guardians, or figurines, modelled on the animal or human world, is never a random choice or merely chosen for decorative effect. Each figurine has an appropriate meaning and is an integral part of the temple building.

One of the most splendid roof guardians is, of course, the dragon: potent symbol of good fortune and power this mythical creature is also attributed with controlling moving bodies of water, such as waterfalls, rivers and seas. Its jewel-like colours and unmistakeable contours are a familiar sight on the George Town skyline.

On ground level, other guardians stand on duty - most notably the lion or fo-dog, carved in stone, and a common feature outside temples. Two particularly fine examples can be seen on the forecourt of the Carpenter's Guild, on Love Lane. They have snarled at newcomers since 1865, when the Guild, largely composed of highly-skilled Cantonese craftsmen, built premises to accommodate a temple and living quarters. For those fresh from China, the Carpenter's Guild was the very first port of call - from here artisans went on to construct many of Malaysia's finest heritage buildings.

The small, charming temple is still known as the 'mother temple' of all Chinese building guilds throughout the country.

Top right: Spectacular roofscape in King Street. The dragons on the roof of the single-storey Tua Pek Kong temple are set against the 'horse-head' gables of the adjacent buildings.

Bottom right: The Carpenter's Guild, Love Lane. Note the faded indigo wall behind the fo-dog - once, much of George Town was lime-washed indigo or ochre. Post-war use of synthetic paints changed both the colour of the city walls and their essential 'breathability.'

Above: Chinese tree shrine.

THE KAPITAN KELING MOSQUE

The foundation stones of this landmark mosque were laid in 1801 on extensive acreage granted by the British to the Muslim section of its East India Company troops. Initially a simple, single-storey building in wood and *atap*, later replaced by brick, the mosque was considerably extended during the early 20th century when onion-shaped domes and sub-domes, turrets, a tall minaret and scalloped archways were added, giving it the characteristics of a splendid Moghul monument. However, in keeping with a tradition that respects and conserves religious buildings, the original corner minarets, diminutively-scaled, can still be seen at the rear of the present mosque.

Inside the mosque, the height of the central prayer hall was doubled during the 1930's, improving ventilation and increasing the source of natural light. As in all mosques, there is little or no furniture on the white marble floors, and walls are left unadorned or subtly decorated with calligraphy and geometric designs. This immaculate interior, with its soaring ceilings and serene atmosphere, allows worshippers to focus whole-heartedly upon their prayers.

And what of the 'Kapitan Keling'? What part of Penang's history does this illustrious name - both that of the mosque and the important street it stands on - refer to?

The word 'kapitan' is a throwback to the pioneer days, when the British administration, ever pragmatic, entrusted each ethnic community to a captain or 'kapitan' of the same race, thus ensuring efficient control and rapid mediation in the event of conflict. When Cauder Mydin Merican was appointed head of the Indian Muslim community, many of whose members came from the Coromandel Coast of South India, of which an early kingdom was called Kalinga, he became known as the Kapitan of the Kelings - as one of the founding fathers of the mosque, the appellation was a means of honouring him.

Today the word 'kapitan' endures in the form of 'curry Kapitan', a delicious *Nyonya* dish made with lashings of coconut milk and tamarind, while 'keling' has fallen into disfavour and is considered politically incorrect. It is unlikely, however, that the word will disappear, given this copper-domed monument in George Town!

Above and left: The Kapitan Keling Mosque, Jalan Masjid Kapitan Keling. The mosque, in Moghul Revival style, has undergone several renovations: the most recent commenced in 2003. On the ground floor of the minaret visitors will find an Islamic Information Centre. Originally, the mosque was surrounded by extensive charity land, intended for the benefit of the Indian Muslim community, but the acreage gradually dwindled as the city became increasingly populated and land was needed for services.

Above and right: *Interior of the Kapitan Keling Mosque. Worshippers find an environment that is always tranquil and conducive to prayer, even during the Friday congregations when the mosque overflows with the faithful or during the celebrations of Hari Raya Aidil Fitri or Hari Raya Haji. Mosque architecture, in general, is dictated by the necessity of a central space large enough for congregational prayer; here, graceful crenellated arches form a colonnade around the vast open prayer hall, cooled by ceiling and floor fans.*

A SUFI SAINT

Muslims from India, for centuries a trading presence in the Malay Archipelago, were among Penang's earliest settlers. They formed a successful business community and, like 'Kapitan Keling', endowed mosques and schools for their Muslim brethren. Some intermarried and assimilated with Malays and became known as '*Jawi Peranakan*' or even 'Penang Malays'.

From India, they bought the tradition of erecting holy shrines and tombs in memory of saints or venerated personalities; today, these shrines provide a quiet, reflective counterpoint to other, more spectacular religious buildings.

On a corner of Chulia Street stands the Nagore Shrine, a delightful Moghul monument in miniature, dating from the early 1800's and still in a fine state of preservation.

Built in honour of a 13th century Sufi mystic, Syed Shahul Hamid, whose gift from God gave him the power to rescue and protect seafaring ships, the shrine was of particular importance to the prosperous Indian Muslims who owned and operated Penang's shipping agencies.

In nearby Leith Street, the Bengali Mosque, built in 1803 for Northern Indian soldiers and farmers, is now a centre for the Tablighi movement. This missionary organisation, of Indian origin, promotes piety within the Muslim community.

Islam was present in the Malay Archipelago from about the 9th century, brought by traders and merchants, and its sources included India, China and the Gulf of Arabia. With the spread of Islam came the allegorical poetry of Sufi teachings, profuse with metaphysics, philosophy and cosmology.

***Left**: The Nagore Shrine. In an alcove embedded in the side of the shrine, artisans make* songkok, *traditional Malay headwear.*

***Above**: The Bengali Mosque.*

***Above left**: The 'keramat' or shrine to Dato Koya, a 19th century miracle worker.*

GODS AND GODDESSES : *The Hindu diaspora*

Above: Intricate tiers of figurines on the gopuram *remind those that enter of both the physical and the ideal world. These tiny sculptures were traditionally carved in stone or fired in terracotta; now they are shaped in cement plaster and painted rainbow hues.*

Right: Gods and goddesses within the temple. Surreal colours and shapes convey the message of an idealised cosmos, embracing all forms of life.

From the 1860's onwards, the ranks of the Indian community in Malaya were swelled by fresh waves of immigrants brought by the British as indentured labour to build towns, roads and public utilities, and later to work in tin mines and on rubber plantations.

The Port of Penang was the main staging post for this migrant flood, and many chose to remain on the island, working on plantations such as Glugor Estate, the legendary dominion of the pioneering Brown family, or staying in George Town where they found port-related jobs or set up myriad businesses and shops.

The majority were Hindu and today Penang possesses over 200 Hindu shrines and temples. Among the oldest is the *Sri Mahamariamman* Temple, situated in the heart of George Town on a site endowed in 1833.

From a simple palm-frond shrine it became, through successive renovations, a colourful masterpiece of Southern Indian temple architecture, constructed, as tradition dictates, to resemble the form of a human body in prone position.

At the main entrance (which corresponds to the 'feet') devotees divest themselves of worldly concerns and pass through the *gopuram*, symbol of the cosmos, whose flat-sided tower features thirty-eight gods and goddesses, four swans and a sculptured mass of brightly-painted decorative detail.

It is worth remembering that Penang's Hindu diaspora was largely composed of young, single men from Southern India. They came with no village or clan ties, no support system to fall back upon, and their working conditions, based on a paternalistic employment system, were often extremely harsh. Family life, if any, lay on the other side of the Indian Ocean. How important, then, the solace of religion!

Today, the *Mahamariamman* Temple is not only a focal point for the Hindu community and its festivals but also an essential part of the vibrant, tumultuous, endearing and unmissable area called 'Little India'.

THE NATTUKKOTTAI CHETTIAR TEMPLE

Right: Passage to the inner sanctuary. The dramatic sweep and strict symmetry of this columned approach is quite different from the colourful medley of many other temples.

Above: Decorative elements are concentrated at ceiling height: dazzling glass chandeliers and brightly painted friezes narrating Hindu epic and legend provide a symbolic counterpoint to the relative austerity at ground level.

In the heart of Little India, within the dim recesses of a temple garage, lies a sacred silver chariot. Once a year, at dawn, it is removed from its Penang Street lair from where, pulled by bulls and accompanied by thousands of devotees, many of them in a state of trance, it begins a long and arduous procession through George Town's streets and suburbs, pausing at every Hindu shrine along the way, until finally, as dusk falls, it reaches its final destination: the Nattukkottai Chettiar Temple in Waterfall Road.

The procession marks the commencement of Thaipusam, a Hindu festival bought from Southern India in the 19th century. It has since metamorphosed into something uniquely Malaysian, assuming local characteristics and attracting huge crowds of non-Hindu onlookers, drawn both by the spiritual magnetism of the event and by the spectacular body piercing and self-immolation of the devotees.

The chariot carries the image of Lord Murugam, protector of the innocent and principal deity of the Nattukkottai Chettiars, patrons of the festival. A mercantile class originating from Tamil Nadu, the Chettiars form one of Penang's historic communities. By tradition bankers and moneylenders, they were central to the development of the Settlement as a commercial hub, providing much of the finance and credit facilities necessary for the newly established shops and trade enterprises.

They still provide these essential services, conducting their business in conventional style whilst tapping into the latest technology. Renowned for a certain frugality in their personal life, the Chettiars are nonetheless astute philanthropists when it comes to religion: their beautifully crafted temples are usually financially well-endowed and rigorously maintained and the Nattukkottai Chettiar Temple in Penang is no exception.

The temple was founded in the mid-19th century on a piece of land bought by the Chettiar community who were already established in Penang Street. Just as in India, the temple complex includes a *chettinar*, or Chettiar living quarters, and a kitchen suitably equipped for nourishing the thousands of worshippers who pass through or even stay during festival periods.

TREE OF LIFE

Left: *Just opposite the Nattukkottai Chettiar Temple in Waterfall Road stands the Sri Meenakshi Sundraeswar Temple founded by the 'bottle' Chettiars, who specialise in the collection and resale of recyclable goods, including, of course, empty bottles. The present temple, completed in 1989, is unique in that it includes lively sculpted images of all the Hindu deities, thus ensuring that each member of this community has the possibility to worship his or her personal deity.*

Above: *Penang abounds with roadside shrines and they all have a special significance. In the middle of life's hectic rush, it is a common sight to see people stopping for a moment beside these shrines to fold their hands together and offer short invocations to their personal gods. Sometimes the shrines develop into temples, with life-sized deities.*

Right: *An image of Krishna hangs in a tree near the Goddess of Mercy Temple, draped with sweet-smelling garlands and surrounded by tiny sticks of joss.*

GRACIOUS LIVING

Visitors to Penang are always struck by the timeless atmosphere of the place; its relaxed, easy pace of life, its heart-warming perpetuation of customs and traditions and its old world charm that contrasts so vividly with the increasingly homogenous, fast-and-furious pace of many other Asian destinations.

Of course, the island has its share of skyscrapers, shopping malls and sophisticated hotels and restaurants - with well over half a million inhabitants, an international airport, excellent infrastructure and a state-of-the-art bridge link to the mainland, this is no sleepy backwater. From all parts of the globe, captains of industry, entrepreneurs, expatriate retirees, writers, artists and intellectuals have chosen to make homes here, attracted as much by the island's comfortable life style, intrinsic beauty and hospitable local population as by the diverse economic advantages.

To the outsider, the Malaysian art of multi-cultural living is a source of endless fascination - with an ethnic mix that is principally Malay, Chinese and Indian, it presents an impressive showcase of ancient and illustrious civilisations. Sometimes these civilisations have blended, creating exotic hybrids such as the Chinese Peranakan and the Jawi Peranakan; sometimes they have retained a distinctly separate identity.

The peoples that make up Penang's diverse cultural heritage each brought their own unique refinements and way of life, reflected, as we have seen, in their religious edifices but also in their dress, cuisine, textiles, furnishings and, perhaps most significantly, the way they built their houses and chose to live in them. Today, this sense of gracious living, of the worthwhile pursuit of an elevated aesthetic, still permeates Penang's vintage buildings, from the towkay's opulent mansion to the wooden kampung home.

Right: A plant-filled inner courtyard situated within a traditional George Town house shows how beautiful effects are often combined with pragmatic considerations. The courtyard, open to the elements, keeps the house airy, cool and light.
Above: Antique furnishings in many Penang houses illustrate East/West eclecticism.

SHOPHOUSES : *The Courtyard Sanctum*

One storey, two storey or even three; lime-washed, stuccoed, ornate or plain - the multi-functional shophouse is a dominant feature of George Town's built heritage and an essential link to connect and unify the richly diverse cityscape.

Early settlers brought this gem of vernacular architecture from the coastal regions of Southern China, where rows of long, narrow houses, sharing a party wall and uniform facades, were a common feature.

Businesses of all kinds could be conducted in the front section of the ground floor, which was completely open to the street, while living areas were located at the rear of the house and the upper floors. Come nightfall, the shopfront was boarded up, and valuables stored in iron vaults.

In Penang, the early 19th century shophouses were low, plain buildings, at first built in timber and then in brick, and roofed with *atap*. Built in rows, back-to-back, connected by their party walls, they maximised the use of available land. As the century progressed these houses, and their more residential version, the terraced house, became increasingly sophisticated, acquiring additional storeys, tiled roofs, and elaborate doorways and windows.

A riot of ornamentation - colourful ceramic shards, rococo plasterwork, intricate carvings and even metal filigree - converged onto narrow, essentially utilitarian facades, reflecting the variety of cross-cultural currents eddying around George Town and its sister cities, Melaka and Singapore. And out of this stylistic whirlpool of Chinese, Malay, Anglo-Indian and European elements a remarkable new decorative form, unique to the Malay Archipelago, evolved: the aptly named Straits Eclectic style.

The row of terraced houses shown here, built in the early 20th century for a Penang family, presents a beautiful, if restrained, example of the Straits Eclectic style. The upper floors feature tall French windows, crowned by fanlights, shaded by wooden louvred shutters, cooled by circular air-vents and embellished with Corinthian pilasters. On the ground level traditional bamboo blinds, or *chiks*, painted green, hang over the arcaded walkway, protecting the houses from the tropical heat and the gaze of passers-by.

Above: *Examples of George Town shophouses, left to right, range from 1840's to 1940's. Features of the facades include louvred shutters, stuccowork, air vents, elaborate doors, coloured tiles, bamboo chiks and, of course, the five-foot way. Despite a growing awareness that these houses have both historic and aesthetic value, many shophouse facades still feature an uneccessary cacophony of highly visible air-conditioning units, unsympathetic plate glass windows and doors, unsuitable paints and garish new signboards.*

The arcaded walkway is a distinctive feature of shophouse architecture. It is known as the 'five-foot way' because of the British administration's specification that all shophouses had to be linked by a verandah-way with a minimum width of five feet. Open to the street, but sheltered from the sun and rain, the 'five-foot way' is an intriguing no-man's land - private in that the shophouse owner tends to use it more or less as he wishes - for the display of goods, as an improvised workshop or even for a quick snooze in a rattan chair - public in that every pedestrian has the right of way.

Once inside the long narrow houses, the world becomes cool, dark and mysterious. A series of semi-open rooms, arranged longitudinally, stretch back into what seems like interminable space. An aperture in the roof lets in light, air and rainwater; the water, flowing down through the air-well, falls into the paved inner courtyard of the ground floor and not only keeps the house cool, but, along with the other elements, ensures a good flow of life force or '*chi* energy'.

Left: Bird's eye view of a street lined with long, narrow shophouses. Note the air-well apertures against the party walls, forming the inner courtyard. Internal windows on the upper floors open onto the air-well. (Larger shophouses often have a central air-well.) Facilities - kitchen, bathroom and open drying area - are located at the rear of the house and a service door opens onto the mandatory back alleyway. Terracotta roof tiles, similar to the Mediterranean version, are increasingly being replaced by galvanised metal.

LINGERING ON THE FIVE-FOOT WAY

The mystery of what lay behind the elaborately carved doors of this Elite shophouse had fascinated me for years. Sometimes the doors would be half open and I could catch the soft glint of the traditional gilded screen, designed to keep prying eyes out of the private workings of the house. (And also, it was said, to allow unmarried Nyonya residents to peep through from within and size up, unnoticed, male visitors.)

I had visited other Peranakan shophouses in George Town and was always impressed by their formidable scale and beauty. However, all too often the contents of these houses had been long dispersed or stored away. Gone, the heavy blackwood chairs, the ornate teak cupboards, the mirrored dressing tables. Gone, too, the display cabinets, the delicate porcelain bowls and coloured figurines. Vanished, a whole way of life.

This house, I knew, was different. Impeccably maintained, with shining coloured tiles on the façade and clean lime-washed walls, it had, nonetheless, probably stopped its clocks in the 1960's. "Would you like to come inside?" asked the lady of the house.

Far left: A fine example of a five-foot way, the arcaded walkway running the length of the shophouse street.
Left: Façade detail of a well-preserved Elite shophouse in Muntri Street. Note the name plaque above the door.

BLACK AND WHITE BLUES

Not all the female inmates of the residential shophouses were the cosseted descendants of patrician *Peranakan* families, destined for marriage and home-making. In the vicinity of Love Lane and Muntri Street, close to their beloved Goddess of Mercy Temple, special sisterhoods of Cantonese *amahs* or maids established their *kongsi* quarters.

From the 1920's onwards, young girls had emigrated from China to escape possible enslavement by a harsh husband or drudgery in the fields and factories. Fiercely independent, they formed sisterhoods to support and protect each other, foreswearing, like nuns, the prospect of marriage and children to enter into a lifetime of service, principally for the Chinese and European elite. Dressed in starched white blouses and flowing black trousers, they epitomised unswerving discipline and loyalty.

The *kongsi* quarters of the affectionately named 'black-and-white' *amahs* served as a convivial base for days-off and, eventually, as a well-organised retirement home - younger *amahs* were always on hand to assist their aged 'sisters'. Today, these courageous feminists have no successors and their community is fast dwindling.

Above: Ah Yeow, one of the last of the black-and-white Cantonese amahs, left China 65 years ago. For 60 years she worked for the same British family; alone now, she awaits return to China.

TILES AND GABLES

Right: Spotting different tiles gracing shophouse facades provides endless amusement. Victorian, Edwardian, Art Nouveau, Art Deco, 1950's mosaic and even 60's op art - all periods are catered for: in fact, quite a few eras can jostle for attention on the same patch of wall.

The tradition of tiling lower facades began with the need to hide rising damp, or to protect walls from water splashing off roads and monsoon drains and from the stream of passers-by along the five-foot way. The Peranakan Chinese elevated this tradition into an art form, mixing unusual colours and patterns to create rich tapestries on their doorsteps. Since many of the tiles were imported from Britain, the English rose is a popular if unlikely motif. Encaustic floor tiles, imported or locally made, are equally colourful.

Left: The shape of gable ends on shophouses and temple buildings are influenced by feng shui and generally signify one of the five elements: curved for water, rounded for wood, smooth for metal, square for earth and spiky for fire. In Penang, their shape could also be related to matters concerning the almanac.

NATURAL VENTILATION

Who needs air conditioning when one can have the world's most attractive house-cooling system? More than just a hole in the wall, the air vent, an integral part of the shophouse ventilation system, is as ingenious as it is beautiful.

Walk down any street in George Town and you will see that each shophouse has its own version of these essential features. Set high up on the wall, on either side of the door and above each ground floor window, their position is calculated to create maximum convection and cross ventilation as they interact with other openings, such as the air-well and inner courtyard.

Carved in wood with a pierced decoration, the air vent is usually painted in auspicious colours or even partially gilded. Look carefully and you will notice that the carved design often includes a central motif with a symbolic meaning. The peony, emblem of wealth and renewal, is a popular motif. The bat brings good luck and happiness. And five bats shown together represent the five blessings: a long life, good health, riches, virtue and a natural death.

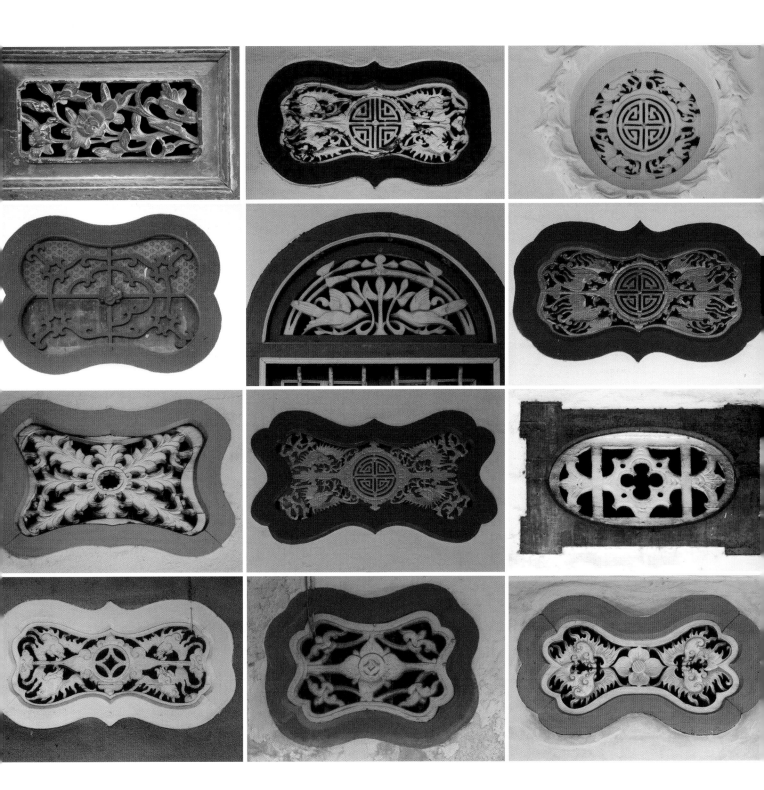

120 ARMENIAN STREET

The historic neighbourhood of Armenian Street is the setting for this beautifully restored house museum, built in the 1870's. Lime-washed walls in indigo and china-green, original 'Peranakan' floor tiles and gilded screens, fully functioning inner courtyards and a coherent selection of period furnishings make for an authentic heritage experience whilst providing inspiration for the variety of uses these traditional houses can fulfil.

Private living and working areas are seamlessly combined with the museum, which includes an exhibition space dedicated to Dr. Sun Yat Sen, 'The Father of modern China'. In 1910 this discreet house, situated in an area notorious for secret societies and hidden escape routes, served as his revolutionary base. From here, the powerful Chinese diaspora was actively targeted for funds, a newspaper was created and the epoch-making 'Penang Conference' was launched. This planned the Canton Uprising, which led to the Xinhai Revolution and the eventual establishment of the Republic of China. At the back of the house the kitchen, equipped with everything from charcoal burners to enamel tiffin carriers, prolongs the refined ambience of the Nyonya household.

TO THE MANSION BORN

The tightly packed density of the shophouse city makes a striking contrast to Penang's diverse array of mansions, villas and bungalows, set like precious ornaments within lush gardens and compounds. Along tree-lined avenues and quiet residential streets, in Pulau Tikus or Jesselton Heights, glimpses of these elegant homes recall what has now become, in other parts of the world, a vanished way of life.

The original British settlers brought to Penang the concept of the Anglo-Indian bungalow, adapting it to the local environment by assimilating elements of the Malay house. Raised off the ground by sturdy pillars - safe, it was hoped, from marauding animals, poisonous insects, monsoon floods and fearsome tropical ills - the bungalow evolved into an airy double-storey structure with deep verandahs, high ceilings and a shady front porch. A covered walkway connected the exterior kitchen and servants' quarters to the main house.

In contrast to the florid public buildings of the late Victorian and Edwardian Empire, colonial bungalows retained an understated charm and discretion. With their plain facades, enlivened in the 1920's by the black-and-white 'mock-Tudor' style, and their sparse interiors, a significant show of affluence came only with the installation of modern plumbing, electric ceiling fans and a humming new refrigerator to replace the icebox…

Members of Penang's early elite - Indian Muslim merchants, Arab traders and Malay Princes - also built houses with a strong Anglo-Indian influence but subtly grafted their own architectural and decorative mannerisms onto austere classical features. Symmetrical facades and strict columns might take their cue from Palladio and Georgian England but expansive verandahs, intricately carved fanlights above tall windows and the graceful arabesques of stucco mouldings spoke of warmer, more exotic climes. A complex web of cultural references spawned differing versions of the 'Straits Eclectic' hybrid style or that *cognoscenti* favourite: 'Sino-Malay-Palladian'.

On the outskirts of George Town's inner city lies Hutton Lane, a clutter of houses, coffee shops and small trades. Footwork and a little patience reveal vestiges of the former 'Muslim Millionaires' Row', grand old houses with sweeping circular driveways and the star and crescent moon traced in plaster on their porticoes.

Above: An example of an early 20th century European house. Note the elevated jack roof, allowing hot air to escape from the upper storey. Some of these houses have been recycled as schools and association premises.

Left, centre: A mansion built for an Indian Muslim merchant.

Top left: Segara Ninda, in upper Penang Road, is an example of Straits Eclectic, Malay style. It has been converted into a small hotel.

Left, bottom: 'Sino-Malay-Palladian.'

Above: A mansion gateway, Jalan Sultan Ahmad Shah.

Bottom right: Château-style 'Woodville', built in 1925, sports a canopy clad in oyster glass and a dome.

Top, far right: Splendid 'Homestead', built in 1919, had its own theatre in the garden.

Top, right: No 32, The Mansion, built in 1926, was inspired by a multitude of European styles and monuments. It is now the beautiful setting for a restaurant.

The most spectacular indication of the vast fortunes made during the late 19th and 20th centuries in tin, rubber or government concessions can be seen in Jalan Sultan Ahmad Shah (formerly Northam Road), where a collection of Chinese *towkay* mansions, dwarfed in some instances by towering sky-scrapers, make for a jaw-dropping architectural and stylistic display.

Minutes from the bustle of central George Town, this coastal stretch was originally favoured by the European community. As they moved further from town Westernised Straits Chinese or *Babas* took up the land, exchanging the traditional shophouse life for the *ang mor lau*, or European villa.

A building extravaganza, which reached its apogee in the 1920's, led to marvellously high-flown interpretations of the French Renaissance château, the Italian palazzo and the English stately home. Domes, towers and cupolas dominated the skyline. Facades dripped with elaborate balustrades, wedding-cake stuccowork and fancy imported glass. Classical statuary and fountains embellished landscaped gardens alongside croquet lawns, tennis courts and the occasional zoo.

Inside the mansions two reception halls - one furnished in Chinese style, the other Western - reflected the *Baba's* curious duality. Formal dining rooms, illuminated by crystal chandeliers, were replete with fine English silver and monogrammed porcelain but the cuisine, one suspects, was usually more rice than roast.

Staff included gardeners, chauffeurs, prized Hainanese cooks and bevies of black-and-white *amahs*. One witty family, it is said, even had that *nec plus ultra*, a British butler. Fortunes were made, lost and made again. Playboy sons raced horses, flew aeroplanes and danced the night away. Pampered *Nyonya* daughters stayed at home, learnt to cook, sew and play the piano. Sumptuous trousseaux were prepared, marriages arranged, dynasties founded.

The Depression and World War II took the gilt off this glittering lifestyle and Malaya's Independence from Britain in 1957 brought changed allegiances and a reappraisal of Western values. By the 1970's, the extended family was a thing of the past, and the staff necessary to run these high-maintenance mansions was increasingly expensive or unavailable. For many, air-conditioned high-rise living was an attractive option.

Mansions were demolished or drifted into ruin. But some still remain, family-owned and proudly resplendent. Others have been restored and given a new lease of life. Restaurants, clubs, and educational centres: mansion life continues, modern style.

THE BLUE MANSION

Not all the Chinese *towkays* chose to build their houses in overtly European style. Hakka millionaire Cheong Fatt Tze's extraordinary indigo-hued mansion on Leith Street speaks loud and clear of 'Old China', despite the lavish use of Western elements within its courtyard interiors.

The mansion's origins date from the late 19th century; unsurprisingly, given the scale of the architecture, the elaborate nature of the decorative details and the perfection of the craftsmanship, it took more than seven long years to complete. An immediate aesthetic appeal belies the mansion's mysteries; its unique features and rarefied Oriental atmosphere never cease to delight and intrigue. And central to an understanding of just why the Blue Mansion differs from neighbouring houses lies its creator's rags-to-riches tale.

A penniless but enterprising adolescent, Cheong Fatt Tze left China for the *Nanyang* in 1856, established himself in Java, married well and within a matter of years, thanks to hard work and a knack with the omnipresent colonial powers, built an empire that straddled Asia and included plantations, real-estate, trade-monopolies, shipping and international banking.

A passion for the good life brought him countless concubines, eight official wives and as many homes. The Blue House in George Town housed Favourite Wife No. 7; it also functioned as an office for the Vice-Consulate of China. In fact, the Sino-traditional style of the mansion reflected the *towkay's* rising star within Chinese officialdom and his unbroken links with the 'mother country'. Unlike many of his Anglicised contemporaries, Cheong Fatt Tze remained pragmatically nationalistic and was instrumental, among other things, in modernising China's industrial and business landscape. In recognition of his unstinting support he was elevated to the rank of Mandarin of the Highest Order.

After his demise in 1916, his estate fell into disarray due to a complicated will, and the mansion hit hard times. By the 1980's, over 30 families were in unofficial 'residence'.

Today, after a prize-winning, Grade 1 restoration, the Blue Mansion represents far more than the sum of its considerable parts: historic house, living museum, gloriously hedonistic place to stay or entertain in, it demonstrates above all what can be achieved with vision, energy and commitment. Not just that of the original owner's but also that of those who saved, restored and made the Mansion live – so graciously - once more!

Left: Forecourt of the recently restored mansion. The red pillars of the second-storey were originally painted this colour to observe the strict colour code of official Chinese residences. Quaint louvred windows show Gothic and Romanesque influence.

Above: Skilled artisans came from China to restore the jewel-like chien nien porcelain shardwork, an outstanding decorative feature of the house. Intricate patterns, figures and flowers are made from breaking and then pasting together fragments of coloured bowls.

Right: The front hall. Heavy blackwood furniture, inlaid with mother-of-pearl, typical of Penang houses, stands on richly coloured Staffordshire tiles. Amazingly, despite decades of abuse and layers of grime - at one time motorbikes, cooking apparatus and workshop tools littered the ground floor - these Victorian tiles remained intact.

Far right, top: In contrast, the original Art Nouveau stained glass panels, dating from the 1890's, were in a desperate state. Missing or broken, they required the formidable expertise of a local restorer with European work experience to return them to their former luminous glory. When the house was built Art Nouveau, with its sinuous, nature-inspired forms, was a completely new decorative style and glasswork, now elevated to an art form, played a central role. Here, in this East/West context, the style is unexpectedly successful and harmonious.

Bottom right: Spiral staircases, in cast iron imported from Scotland, link the outer wings to the upper floors.

Left: Simpler in style than the elaborate central areas, the outer wings are paved with hexagonal terracotta tiles from China.

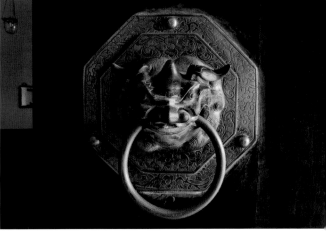

Left: Through the open roof light and shadow dance onto the delicate filigree of the upper floor verandahs overlooking the central courtyard area. In keeping with the highly eclectic nature of the mansion, Victorian cast ironwork, manufactured at the MacFarlane's foundry in Scotland, is surmounted by Chinese lattice screens, carved in timber. Elderly Cantonese craftsmen from Penang were responsible for the repair and replacement of the timberwork found throughout the house, their age-old, fast-disappearing skills complemented by the use of traditional tools.

The interior courtyards, five in all, open to the sky, the wind, the sun and the cooling rain, are an essential part of the mansion's inner workings. They also demonstrate the important role played by feng shui in a wide range of Penang constructions. The great lengths that Cheong Fatt Tze went to in order to fulfil feng shui principles when building his mansion make a fascinating study.

Top right: Carved and gilded screens, sensitively restored, keep evil spirits at bay.

Bottom right: An auspicious bat-motif front door handle, cast in bronze, brings good fortune to the entrance of the house.

THE SEA REMEMBRANCE STORE

Above: Street-side, the mansion boasts ornate gilded doors, decorative air vents and one of George Town's grandest five-foot ways. The adjoining temple, secluded behind magnificent ironwork gates, was built by Chung Keng Kwee and served both as ancestral hall and family school.

Right: A view through the mansion's front entrance into the central courtyard.

Far Right: Both the mansion and the temple contain museum-quality gilded woodcarvings, executed by Cantonese craftsmen.

The British, who considered them a threat, called them 'secret societies'. To their Chinese members, they were 'welfare associations'. Whatever the correct definition, by the mid-19th century the Hakka-dominated Hai San society was one of the most powerful of these subterranean organisations, a driving force behind Malaya's burgeoning tin industry and comptroller for the huge labour forces needed to mine the precious ore.

Against a background of warring factions and bloody feuds, great fortunes were made in mainland Perak's tin mines and inevitably these riches found their way to Penang where extravagantly eccentric lifestyles were the norm.

The Sea Remembrance Store, an opulent courtyard mansion with an astonishing private temple attached, was built by the former leader of the Hai San, Chung Keng Kwee, shortly after the British prohibited secret societies in 1890. (Well before this, in a conciliatory manner, the British had appointed the secret society leader 'Kapitan China' after his peacekeeping role in the Perak-based, tin-fuelled, Larut Wars).

The Kapitan erected his poetically named mansion on George Town's Church Street, in the place of property acquired from his erstwhile rivals, the Cantonese-dominated Ghee Hin society. A relatively sober exterior, painted in pastel shades and enhanced by a graceful cast-iron balcony, invites comparison with the flamboyant Blue Mansion, built at around the same time by fellow Hakka Cheong Fatt Tze.

Inside the Church Street house, similarities in the choice of imported materials - the Staffordshire floor tiles and the cast-iron columns from MacFarlane, which support, as at the Blue Mansion, a metal filigreed verandah overlooking the central courtyard - lead one to assume that the two tycoons must have exchanged a few decorating tips in their spare time.

That aside, the conception of the two houses was in fact very different. Whereas the Blue Mansion remains firmly rooted in a romantic 19th century ideal, the Sea Remembrance Store aspires quite plainly, in terms of layout, domestic logistics and atmosphere, towards the cusp of the 20th century. Meticulously restored, the Store has now become 'The Pinang Peranakan Mansion' and is open for visits.

Top left: A detail of the unusual roof decorations on the Chung Keng Kwee Temple. Mythological creatures, cast from moulds, gambol amongst a tumult of decorative detail and organic images. An imitation of blue coral is particularly beautiful.

Bottom left: Inside the temple, walls are decorated with a unique series of three-dimensional tableaux, in sculptured, subtly coloured ceramic. Still-life theatres in miniature, these tableaux, with their 'cast' of tiny figures, depict scenes from Chinese legend and heroic drama.

Central left: A corner of the principal courtyard area includes a cast-iron column, one of several, manufactured by MacFarlane's foundry in Scotland. Victorian encaustic floor tiles are from Staffordshire, England. In true Straits Eclectic style, fleur-de-lys motifs on the staircase contrast with traditional Chinese doors.

Right: The mansion has now been furnished to portray a typical Peranakan *interior*. The finery of the bridal chamber, with filtered red light and formal furnishings, indicates the ceremonial and symbolic importance of the Chinese wedding. Downstairs, a Western-style dining-room features coloured glass epergnes and the obligatory sideboard.

THE URBAN VILLAGE

Traditional habitations in and around George Town are not restricted to the bricks and mortar of the Chinese shophouse or mansion. Other forms of housing, wholly or partially in timber, are also visible but, being less resistant to extreme climatic conditions, the implacable march of white ant and easily destroyed in the event of fire, they are now few and far between.

Those remaining provide not just an appealing contrast to the masonry rigour of the shophouse city but also give an indication of how, once upon a time, these areas were *kampungs*, villages surrounded by gardens and tracts of agricultural land. Indeed, a 1798 plan of George Town shows extensive paddy fields in the area that would soon become Leith Street and, later, the Hakka Millionaires' Row.

The same plan also shows the presence of a 'Malay Town', situated to the south of Acheen Street, with two mosques close by. Today, the name 'Malay Street' provides a hint as to what this area once was, although orderly shophouses lining the street have long replaced the *kampung* houses and their verdant environs.

Within George Town material proof of the existence of these villages is often to be found in evocative street names - *Kampung* Malabar, *Kampung* Deli, *Kampung* Kaka - and these names, in turn, reflect the ethnic group to which the *kampung* inhabitants belonged.

Malays, Indians, Sumatrans and Arabs - for this predominantly Muslim population, the village evolved around the mosque, and inhabitants of the village formed an integral part of both the secular and religious community.

Although sharing common religious beliefs and social mores, each ethnic group brought, nonetheless, their own distinctive culture and aesthetic, and this was reflected in the conception of their houses and the decorative detailing.

Inevitably, the city encroached upon these villages. Today, finding traces of them hidden in the dense city fabric is akin to a frustrating treasure-hunt - there are still clues to be followed but the prizes are often out of grasp. A house standing yesterday may be gone today, a community fragmented, old traditions forgotten or abandoned.

And yet, despite rampant development and rapidly changing lifestyles, fragile vestiges of these urbanised villages still remain, the temporal nature of their houses invested with a poignant beauty.

Above: This charming wooden house stands in Kampung Syed, an urban village just off Burmah Road, whose inhabitants were originally part of Penang's small but influential Arab trading community. Luxurious high-rise living provides the 'backdrop architecture' for the enclave.

Right: Examples of well-preserved urban Malay houses, set in greenery. Note the full-length windows and fine carvings of the fanlights. Corrugated metal has replaced the atap roofs.

PULAU TIKUS

Catholic Eurasians, fleeing religious persecution, were amongst the earliest settlers of Penang. Like the Europeans, they eventually left their initial inner city habitat, and joined other Eurasians in what is now the up-market suburb of Pulau Tikus. There they built attractive bungalows in Anglo-Malay style, raised from the ground by masonry pillars and set in spacious gardens. Louvred shutters filtered the sun and airy verandahs created outside/inside living space.

Although a small community, the Eurasians played, and still play, a significant role in the field of economy, education and music. Family names and culinary specialities recall distant Portuguese connections and contribute to Penang's many-layered diversity. The whole area of Pulau Tikus was known as Kampung Serani, or Eurasian Village, despite the fact that other communities settled there and built houses of a similar style.

Left: *This highly decorative bungalow was originally inhabited by a Jewish family.*

Right: *An Arab's bungalow.*

Top, far right: *The gold stupa of the Thai Temple reminds us of the Siamese community who settled here during Francis Light's era.*

RASHID, A GEORGE TOWN STORY

Abdul Rashid Stephen bin Abdullah was originally baptised Stephen Laing, of Portuguese-Eurasian and Scottish parentage. George Town born and bred, Rashid attended a Catholic mission school, run by French brothers. A convert to Islam, he changed his name accordingly. Later, he married Luwie, an Iban from Sarawak.

***Left**: During the day, Rashid pedals his trishaw through the streets of George Town, streets he says he knows 'like the back of my hand'. In the evening he can be found in the vicinity of Penang Road, helping Luwie make the best satay in town.*

***Top right**: Rashid and Luwie live in Kedah Road, in what was a former Jawi Peranakan, or Penang Malay neighbourhood. Their abode is in one of my favourite George Town houses - beloved not because it is grand or highly decorated but because it, and its adjoining twin, are charming curiosities. Possibly built by Indians, their proportions and certain details are quite different from the nearby shophouses. Rather like Rashid, they defy definition.*

***Bottom left**: Inside, the house is spick and span and full of love.*

JAZZ AGE AND BEYOND

Modernism in architecture came relatively late to Penang, delayed by financial crashes, the Second World War and a pragmatic reluctance to break away from the tried and tested. After all, given climatic conditions, who would want to improve upon the cool courtyard shophouse or the airy bungalow?

Pre-war, the clean rectilinear lines and simplified ornamentation of Art Deco marked a significant departure from the exotically hybrid Classicism so prevalent in Penang. It was a style taken up by the adventurous or the newly rich; in George Town examples of the Art Deco style can be seen on the facades of shophouses, hotels and commercial buildings (the interiors invariably revert back to a more traditional aesthetic) often faced in Shanghai plaster, a weatherproof material which gives the appearance of sculpted stone.

It was not until the 1950's and 60's that new building methods and materials really filtered through and made the transition to the Bauhaus-inspired International Style. Innovative use of glass, metal and plastic, advances made in concrete technology and rapid urbanisation all heralded the way for contemporary architecture. Increasing use of air conditioning was another important factor in the changing face of tropical countries such as Malaysia. Ironically, in a post-colonial era, its immediate benefits in terms of physical comfort also brought a Western-influenced design language with little chance of cooling the building by natural means. Many buildings were conceived with no reference to tropical living and a total disregard of their environmental impact.

Since the 1970's, the construction of several radical and thought-provoking buildings has engaged Penangites in a meaningful debate on how they see the future of their built heritage. George Town's 65 storey KOMTAR built in 1973 by Datuk Lim Chong Keat, with a Buckminster Fuller geodesic dome, the sculptural Penang State Mosque, built in 1979 and inspired by Oscar Niemeyer, and Ken Yeang's 1998 bio-climatic UMNO Tower have all, in their different ways, changed the island's horizons, both visually and intellectually.

A small collection of Modernist gems are scattered around the suburban villadom of outer George Town, a startling and amusing contrast to the stately homes of the towkays.

Left: *This 1950's house makes playful reference to the ocean-liner, with its curved facades, sun decks, iron railings, rows of portholes and circular air vents.*

Above: *A later, upbeat version. Note the car porch, 'flying buttress' window shades and jazzy metalwork.*

SPOTLIGHT

A landmark of Art Deco architecture, the Rex Cinema on Burmah Road, shown right, was built in 1939. It was the island's first air-conditioned cinema and generations of Penangites fondly remember the discomfort of its seats (first and second class), the deafening roar of its audio system and, most importantly, the fact that tasty meals could be smuggled into the screening from the hawker stalls so conveniently stationed outside.

Post-war, the cinema was operated by the Shaw Brothers, Sir Run Run and Sir Runme, Asia's answer to the Hollywood Kordas. In Penang their entertainment empire included two amusement parks, the New World and the Old World, featuring Teochew and Cantonese opera, dodgem cars and Rose Chan, a lightly-clad lady who wrestled with snakes.

Reminders of the raffish 50's and 60's, when duty-free Penang was a popular resort for soldiers, sailors and good-time girls, have not totally disappeared: faded advertisements for cha-cha and rumba lessons, photographs of improbably bouffant hairstyles in perm parlour windows or the still thriving Hong Kong Bar in Chulia Street send the nostalgic traveller whistling back in time.

ENCORE!

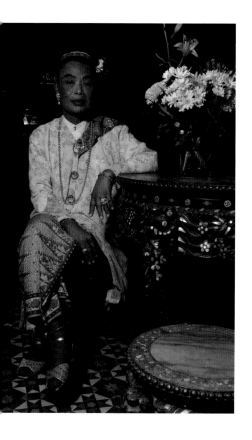

'Baba Nyonya intimate theatre'. An outstanding performance by Mohd Bahroodin Ahmad at 120 Armenian Street.

The actor, in his consummate role as Nyonya matriarch Bibik Hitam, enlivens and preserves local history and traditions, affectionately transforming the idiosyncrasies of the different cultural communities into artistic expression.

Before the advent of the cinema, special forms of theatre, in particular *Boria* and *Bangsawan*, were highly popular with Penang audiences. *Bangsawan*, musical dramas brought originally from India, and then 'Malayanized,' held universal appeal for Penang's multi-ethnic communities. A *Bangsawan* troupe could include as many as fifty people, with the female roles played by men and a supporting cast made up of Malays, *Baba* Chinese and Indians. The theatre's spontaneous style can be compared to the Italian *commedia dell'arte*.

Leading exponent of *Bangsawan* and *Boria* is Penang's 'Living Heritage Treasure' Mohd Bahroodin Ahmad (shown left), otherwise known as Cikgu Baha, a veteran performance artist, oral historian, teacher, choreographer and promoter of local performing arts.

Left: *The Rex Cinema, Burmah Road, built pre-war in pure Art Deco style.*
Above: *The Shaw brothers talent-spotted Malay singer and actor P. Ramlee in Penang in 1948; he went on to make dozens of films for their studios and recorded hundreds of songs. The late P. Ramlee is considered one of Malaysia's best-loved entertainers.*

ISLANDER

"The island of Pinang with its lofty peak, dense woods, and shores fringed with palms sheltering Malay Kampungs, each with its prahus drawn up on the beach, looks impressive enough … a brilliant place under a brilliant sky."

Thus wrote the indomitable lady explorer Isabella L. Bird, in her 1879 travelogue 'The Golden Chersonese and the way thither'. Today, on the northern coast of the island, the palm trees are still omnipresent but many of the kampungs she mentions have made way for luxurious beach hotels and residential condominiums, while to the south housing estates and a flourishing industrial zone have been developed on former plantations and paddy fields.

A glance at an aerial view of the island (see page 150) indicates, however, that a large expanse of the central and western side of the island remains swathed in a vivid jungly green, dotted here and there with long-established farming and fishing communities.

Caught up in the urban excitement of George Town and its environs it is easy to forget that another side of the island exists, where life moves at a slower, quieter pace and scenic beauty takes centre stage. Coastal and hill vistas replace the architectural sights: in their absence we marvel at the wildlife which ranges from rare butterflies to long-tailed macaques, whilst dazzling plants and flowers remind us that this is a part of the world renowned for its extraordinary biodiversity.

The landscape is peopled by fruit farmers, fishermen or agricultural smallholders, villagers still nourished by local produce, living in harmony with Nature and her bounty. Their timber houses, too, built from sustainable regional woods, using time-honoured methods, reflect this precious ethic.

Right: Animated conversation in the main street of a fishing village. Outside the timber house, an array of shoes and slippers reminds us of the wise Asian practice: 'No outdoor footwear in the house'.

THE KAMPUNG IDYLL

First-time visitors to the Malay kampung are struck by the lack of physical boundaries: here, no walls or fences proclaim jealously-guarded individual possession; instead, each householder is linked to his neighbour by an open path and, just as importantly, has an innate understanding of what makes communal life work. The concept of sharing and solidarity, hallmarks of the Malay way of life, means that modern-day ills of isolation and alienation have no place in the kampung, for each individual, however modest, is a respected member of the wider community.

The design of the Malay house, with its open spaces, minimal partitions and hospitably wide verandahs, also demonstrates this notion of informal fraternity, whilst the provision of a private space for the female members of the household ensures that religious and social customs are observed.

The houses shown here, situated in the environs of Balik Pulau, illustrate the charm and practicality of Malay vernacular architecture. Constructed by local carpenters, using the post-and-beam technique, and incorporating readily available materials, the flexible, modular design allows for easy assemblage.

THE VILLAGE BARBER

Left: Apart from the mosque, the most important public space in this village is Hashim's barber shop where, over the years, generations of local menfolk have exchanged greetings, relaxed, read the newspaper… and had their hair cut. The shop features spotless white drapes, photographs of singer and actor P. Ramlee and a convivial metal swing.

Centre right: Hashim lives close to his barber shop with his wife Rokiah, in a house built by his family over a century ago. Unusually, it still retains its attractive and heat resistant atap roof, made from split palm fronds: due to atap's relatively high-maintenance and limited availability, most Malay houses now have roofs of galvanised iron.

Bottom right: The compact, immaculate and well-organized kitchen is typical of the Malay household. Note the rectangular betel chewing set on the lower shelf. Of great symbolic import, betel is offered to guests in a domestic context as a token of friendship and esteem.

Top right: Upstairs, full length windows and open lattice work (the same as in the barber shop) keep sleeping quarters cool and airy.

BERGUMBIRA

Floral, geometric or just plain ebullient - fretwork decoration on Malay kampung houses is a design language that speaks to the heart. Wooden panels carved to resemble lace or sunbursts, open porches with balustrades that seem to dance, wild and abundant foliage, owing more to the carpenter's skills than to nature: these houses have a joyful refinement that belies their rural village environs.

The fretwork, hand-tooled by local craftsmen or by the house owner himself, is not just there to beautify a façade; it serves as a vital component in solving one of the major concerns of life in the tropics: keeping cool. A multitude of perforations, coupled with adjustable louvred windows, ensure a constant flow of air. Perforated wooden boards behind the shuttered windows are decorative and also ensure safety.

When night falls, the interior light passes through the fretwork, creating patterns and silhouettes, recalling wayang kulit, or shadow play.

***Right and left**: Examples of fretwork found on houses near the market town of Balik Pulau, on the western side of the island. The loved-or-loathed durian fruit is a local speciality.*

403
MUKIM E

KAMPUNG MELAYU, Ayer Itam Road

Stay long enough in Penang and you will start to see that many places, separated by geographical location, are closely linked by a shared history.

Top, far left: Builders from India were commissioned to erect this domed mausoleum in Kampung Melayu to house the tomb of Sheikh Omar Basheer (d. 1881), the 19th century imam, Sufi mystic and reformist, whose origins can be traced to Hadhramout (Yemen).

The Sheikh's descendants are still connected to the Acheen Street Mosque enclave in inner city George Town (see page 28).

Bottom and top left: Next to the mausoleum stands Sheikh Basheer's country house, which is lovingly maintained by his family.

Right: The very special atmosphere of the house, with its green painted walls hung with framed portraits of distinguished family members, provides a link to those early pioneering days of Penang, when Muslim settlers, of Arab and Acehnese descent, wrote an important chapter in the island's history book. Today, Ayer Itam is synonymous with the Kek Lok Si Temple, Malaysia's largest temple complex, built in 1905 and partially sponsored by Cheong Fatt Tze (page 86).

SEA BREEZE

Although the story of Penang is closely linked to the sea, it was not until the early 20th century that the beautiful coastline to the north of George Town and Pulau Tikus was perceived as viable terrain for a particular form of development, unrelated to trading or fishing activities. The notion of the 'seaside resort' and the pursuit of fashionable leisure activities such as swimming, sailing and rowing slowly trickled out from Europe, manifesting itself here and there in the form of the odd beach bungalow, but most of those who could afford to indulge in playtime pursuits preferred the cooler climes and country walks of Penang Hill.

An impetus came in 1903 when a group of young Europeans established the Penang Swimming Club in Tanjung Bungah, 'the Flower Coast'. A clubhouse and a diving tower were tucked into a 'charming little bay, hemmed in by fantastic rocks, and half hidden by varied tropical foliage'; by the 1930's, a pavilion had been built for Ladies and Children (in true British style, they were barred from the clubhouse) and an Olympic-sized salt water swimming pool rose majestically up from the beach.

Holiday bungalows became the norm - even the Light Street Convent acquired property in Tanjung Bungah, to the delight of the nuns and pupils - as beach life became increasingly popular. This was encouraged, no doubt, not just by the vogue for water sports but also by a radical, Coco Chanel-inspired change in fashion, which led to Western, or Westernised, ladies escaping the prison of corsetry, adopting informal dress and sporting a suntan.

Post World War II, a traveller writes of 'Tanjung Bungah, bristling with cafes, restaurants and bungalows. Here is the week-end centre for the sea-loving George Town residents and their outstation friends'. Further along the coast, at Batu Ferringhi, the 'Lone Pine' Hotel became a firm favourite for these 'outstation' visitors and also for locally-based Europeans who came for Sunday curry *tiffin*, sea-bathing or a stroll under the *casuarina* trees and, for the children, the entrancing tricks of the Indian snake charmer.

Above: On the north coast, tranquil fishing villages and kampungs make way for lively beach resorts and apartment blocks.

Left: The winding coastal road to Batu Ferringhi conceals some lovely surprises: hidden coves and beach houses built in all sorts of styles - Anglo-Malay, Hollywood Mogul, 50's Cabana. This unusual house is in a style all of its own.

A VIEW FROM THE VERANDA

Closer to town, the area of Gurney Drive was also a prime location for seaside villas and recreation. Penangites came from all over the island to enjoy the sandy beach and wide promenades, ideal for early morning exercise or evening walks enhanced by spectacular sunsets and the joyous anarchy of hawker stands lining the sea front.

Today, high-rises overshadow the remaining bungalows and sidewalk cafes, gleaming shopping malls vie with the sunsets, and the hawker stands have been corralled, for sanitary reasons, into a municipal precinct. Fortunately, this has not affected the friendly local atmosphere and the area remains a 'gourmet destination'.

Considered one of Penang's most well-known and prestigious addresses, Gurney Drive is named after Sir Henry Gurney, British High Commissioner for the Federation of Malaya, who was assassinated in 1951 during the 12 year armed struggle with Communist insurgents that the British called, somewhat euphemistically, 'The Emergency'.

Since Penang Island was not directly caught up in the guerrilla warfare, some of the European rubber planters who were at risk on isolated estates sent their wives and children to Penang for safety, and as a result a school was founded on Penang Hill. Later, 'Uplands' wended its way down to the environs of Gurney Drive, and from there to Batu Ferringhi where it flourishes in the 21st century as a well-regarded international school.

The most important event during the Emergency years was the negotiation of independence from Britain, under the leadership of Tunku Abdul Rahman, seventh son of the Sultan of Kedah and a former pupil of Penang Free School. On August 31st, 1957, the Independent Federation of Malaya was established, with the Tunku as the first Prime Minister. In 1963 the Federation of Malaya became Malaysia.

In the years since Independence a commodity-based economy has successfully diversified into manufacturing, services and tourism. By 2020 Malaysia aims to achieve a fully developed nation status. In Penang, the 31st August *Merdeka* Day celebrations, commemorating the end of colonial domination and the birth of a new nation, are celebrated on the Esplanade.

Above: Most splendid of all the seaside residences is the Loke Villa. a tropical marriage of Arts and Crafts country house and Italianate villa, designed in 1924 by Scottish architect David McLeod Craik, (For the full visual effect of this see pg 64.)
Left: Verandah in typical bungalow style.

THE ARTIST'S EYE

It took the talent and energy of Malaysian artist Rebecca Duckett-Wilkinson and her husband to transform a heritage mansion into a stunning contemporary home, suitable for informal family life and relaxed entertaining. The happy transition was achieved without impinging on the mansion's aesthetic integrity: no structural changes were made nor foolhardy attempts to create an air-conditioned habitat. Instead, the house respects the original design intention, allowing the flow of fresh sea breezes through numerous doors and windows. Castle height ceilings, embellished with strap work, and the cool glazed surface of vintage wall-tiles, keep temperatures down as well as providing visual impact. The artist's strong palette, inspired by the brilliance of tropical colour and nature, and her background in textile design, are reflected in the creative use of rainbow-hued fabrics, whilst an imaginative and uncontrived mix of furnishings and artefacts demonstrate a real love and knowledge of Asian crafts. Even the neo-baroque pattern of the English wall tiles, a marvellous but potentially overpowering decorative feature, is effortlessly woven into the harmonious East-meets-West, past-meets-present final effect.

GREEN POWER

The ancient rainforests, jungles and mangrove swamps of Malaysia possess one of the world's most diverse terrestrial ecosystems and shelter some of the more beautiful, bizarre and improbable organisms on the planet. Yet the fragile nature of this priceless treasure is under constant threat - contraband wildlife trade, illegal and unsustainable logging, erosion and indiscriminate tourism, coupled with the insidious impact of climatic changes and a globalised, industry-driven 'throw-away' culture, are just some of the factors that could herald its tragic demise.

Malaysia is fortunate, however, to have both a government and committed activist groups that recognise the interdependence of man and his environment and the urgent need to protect and maintain an ecological balance. Strict legislation and its implementation limits potential damage; the development of eco-awareness programmes seeks to engage the individual; an ongoing

Above: Fragrant flowers of the Cannonball tree blossom in the Penang Botanic Gardens. Unconnected to foliage, these flowers grow directly from the tree trunk. Believed to have been introduced from South America in the late 19th century, the tree is an example of the important exchange of botanical specimens occurring during the colonial era between the two great rainforest regions.
Right: Landscaped gardens at the Kek Lok Si Temple, or Temple of Supreme Bliss, in Ayer Itam.

dialogue with the developed world (lesson-giver yet voracious consumer of tropical woods and by-products) encourages international solidarity: all these initiatives will, hopefully, bear fruits for the future.

For the visitor wishing to explore Malaysia's natural wonders, responsible eco-tourism, which seeks to substantially reduce the negative impact of tourism upon the environment, is now a mainstream option. Carefully controlled national parks and marine reserves propose a first-hand nature experience and the possibility to bond with an awesome universe. Although Penang is not the obvious choice for the more adventurous nature lover she offers, nevertheless, a wealth of opportunities for discovering regional flora and fauna. And be warned: hikers can still get lost in her dense jungle and hill forests. In 2003, Penang's 'last wilderness' was proclaimed a National Park. Located on the northwest coast near the fishing village of Teluk Bahang, the park includes virgin jungle, mangrove forests and a meromictic lake. This unusual seasonal phenomenon occurs when freshwater monsoon rains lie suspended above saline seawater, creating a dual water lake. Penang's Butterfly Farm, Reptile House or Bird Park also give a fascinating peek at some of the vulnerable creatures who share our planet.

THE PENANG BOTANIC GARDENS

It was a long time before I realised that the Botanic Gardens and the Waterfall Gardens were one and the same. The reason was simple: the initial attraction of the gardens, established in 1884, was in fact the Waterfall, which had been incorporated within the landscaped site; eventually the vertiginous cascades were declared out of bounds to the general public but the 'Waterfall' moniker lingered on and its copious waters continue to irrigate one of Penang's most beloved attractions.

The Gardens replaced earlier gardens in the Ayer Itam area, and were not conceived to be mere pleasure grounds: their *raison d'être* was principally linked to colonial economic aspirations. Thousands of seedlings from all over the globe were imported here, successfully cultivated or abandoned, possessively guarded or exported *en masse*. Along with the Botanic Gardens in Singapore, this was where the administration stocked and propagated rare tropical plants and commercial crops: fruits, spices and, most importantly, the rubber tree.

Rubber tree saplings, germinated in Britain's Kew Gardens from seeds smuggled out of the Amazon, arrived in Malaya in 1888; just three decades later *hevea* had become the *sine qua non* of a booming economy and the source of many Penang fortunes.

The layout of the Botanic Gardens was assigned to its first Superintendent, Charles Curtis. He made remarkable use of the natural landscape to create the green haven we see today; an ideal park, complete with Fern House and frog-filled Lily Pond, for nature lovers, joggers and gregarious monkeys.

Left: Pavilion in the Formal Garden. This area, with its colourful borders of flowering and foliage plants, was created in 1936 to resemble the classic English garden. It now also incorporates a distinctive Malaysian identity.
Above: Garden of the Governor's Residence, planted by the same Gardens Department.

THE TROPICAL SPICE GARDENS

Right: *Just past the beach resort of Batu Ferringhi lie the Tropical Spice Gardens, where a former rubber plantation has been converted into one of the most delightful and innovative gardens in the region. Opened to the public in 2003, the garden's lush vegetation, planted on landscaped terraces, attests to the lightning speed of tropical growth and the presence of a natural waterfall. A series of themed trails both enchant and inform the visitor: the fragrant Spice Trail, for example, features over 100 varieties of spice and herb plants, including nutmeg and cinnamon, and is enriched by a visit to the on-site Spice Museum, which relates the history of spice and how spices are produced and processed. Old architectural elements recycled as garden features, hammocks secured to trees for the weary, a giant swing for the young (and the young-at-heart) and a stylish café with superb sea views all speak of the love and care that went into this privately-funded initiative.*

Left: *Just some of the unusual flowers and decorative plants to be found in Penang.*

PENANG HILL

Among the more charming legacies of the British colonialists figure the picturesque hill stations that still exist amidst Malaysia's highland territory, much to the delight of Western travellers in search of nostalgia. The *Ye Olde* ambience of country lanes, tea kiosks and neat flower-filled gardens coupled with tropical jungle sights and sounds has a surreal attraction; the cosiness of half-timbered bungalows, many still in pristine condition, completes the exotic yet homely picture.

Oldest of these hill stations is that of Penang Hill, established in the late 18th century, 830 metres above sea level. Like its grander counterparts in British India, it was conceived as a cool escape from the debilitating heat of the lowlands and the threat of malaria; one of its earliest buildings, unsurprisingly, was the Convalescent Bungalow.

Penang Hill, or 'Bukit Bendera', was popularised by early paintings and engravings and became a favourite haunt of walkers, botanists and those in search of truly spectacular views. Visitors made the ascent on Sumatran ponies or were carried in sedan chairs, one passenger for six bearers.

The funicular train service, successfully launched in 1923, led to a sharp increase in residential development, although the shameful exclusion policy practised in British social and sporting clubs extended to the Hill - the upper slopes were reserved for Europeans, whilst wealthy locals were allocated the lower slopes. Impervious, Chinese *towkays* built splendid 'country' villas - named them 'Great Wall' or 'Mon Séjour' - in cock-a-snoot contrast to the understated bungalows - 'Fern Cottage' and 'Woodlands' - of the lofty colonial masters.

The 'mems' and 'tuans' are now long gone but the 'Little England' atmosphere lingers on. Roses still bloom in this dreamy Arcadia and the menu at the Bellevue Hotel continues to feature that colonial favourite 'inchi kabin'.

'The Best View of Penang'. A quintessential hill station house and terraced garden complete with clipped hedges, immaculate lawns and flowerbeds overflowing with roses and hydrangeas. Picket fences, English cast-iron garden furniture - just right for tea and scones - and a weather vane atop the chimney provide the finishing touch.

HOUSE
AND GARDEN

Left: *The birthplace house of popular entertainer P. Ramlee has been reconstructed in the same locality, adjacent to a perfoming arts complex dedicated to his memory. For the foreign visitor, the house and its furnishings give an indication of a typical* kampung *interior of the pre-war period. Photographs and personal posessions, including the performer's violin, give an added resonance. The kitchen, as compact as that of a boat, contains an interesting selection of utensils.*

Outside, the sober greenery of low clipped hedges complement the pots of flamboyant bougainvillea and hibiscus, or 'Bunga Raya', Malaysia's National Flower. Under the house, an old bicycle bears witness to a bygone era, when Penang's roads were quiet, shady thoroughfares suitable for cyclists and walkers.

Near right, top: *The perfumed frangipani tree.*

Far right, top: *A garden is not a garden without a cat or two! Penang cats are special - often ginger, with strange kinked tails.*

Bottom: *A Malay house is surrounded by a typically lush garden.*

URBAN GARDENS

Right: *Cleared of the flotsam of everyday life, the five-foot way becomes an urban garden, the Oriental equivalent of the Western window box. Bamboo and palms, surprisingly sturdy in small earthenware pots, luminous green ferns and brilliant flowering plants are reminders that even in George Town, the jungle and its treasures are never far away.*

The shrill screech of birds, emanating from closed-up shophouses, can be misleading - this is not a new form of inner city wildlife but signals the presence of a 'Swiftlet Hotel' - an empty house transformed into a makeshift factory for the production of birds' nests. The bird noise is actually a recording, acting as an ingenious magnet for the birds that will fly in and produce the Chinese delicacy.

Left: *A modern take on the five-foot way. In a quiet corner of George Town a florist shows how, with imagination and style, a traditional shophouse can make the transition into the 21st century.*

THE SPICE OF LIFE

As our journey through Penang's rich heritage draws to a close, we pause to consider the astonishing diversity of all we have seen. Ethnic enclave, urban shophouse, vintage colonial - the buildings of Penang reflect and enhance her illustrious trading past, a past whose roots were fed and nurtured, so many centuries ago, by a tiny yet vital ingredient: spice.

It was the quest for spices that brought merchants and traders to the Malay Archipelago, creating links with the great ports across the expanding world, opening trade routes, inspiring explorers, and kindling brutal wars. Spices brought Arab, Indian and Chinese traders, who settled and assimilated with the local Malays. Spices brought the Portuguese, the Dutch and then the British, colonial powers who stayed long enough to leave diversely appreciated traces. In Penang, spices made great fortunes, financed mansions and palatial lifestyles, tamed and shaped rural areas into lucrative plantations and provided work for new immigrants.

Spices no longer play a role in world economies, centuries have passed since peppercorns were valid tender to pay the rent, but the varied and delectable cuisine of Penang, whose many dishes bear the fragrance of locally grown spices, still connects us to this epic story. The Indian, Malay, Chinese, Eurasian and Nyonya kitchen all excel in the subtle and inventive use of the roots, leaves, fruits, seeds and nuts which, by their exotic, aromatic and sometimes delicately obscure nature, are loosely defined as spices.

Thailand's proximity has also enriched Penang's palate, giving Nyonya cooking - that distinctive, sophisticated blend of Chinese and Malay ingredients and flavours - an added zing with tamarind and lime. Fusion food, at its best.

Left and above: Nyonya cooking can involve painstaking preparation, which might account for its slide into obscurity some years back. Happily, an increasing number of restaurants now feature this cuisine, with dishes such as otak-otak, beef rendang and sambal petai.

SUGAR AND SPICE

And all things nice...

Left*: If you want to try your hand at Malaysian dishes, then Little India in George Town is the place for finding all the dried spices you will need. Chances are, you will come away with more than just spices - swept up by the gay explosion of music blasting out from every open shop front, you will be suddenly tempted by colourful saris, exotic perfumes, brassware and bangles.*

A pause for refreshment should include a 'banana leaf curry' - curry served on a strip of banana leaf or that Malaysian favourite, roti canai - flattened discs of feather-light dough, prepared to order, fried in ghee until golden-brown, accompanied by spicy sauce.

Near left*: Bowls of spices in Little India show cardamom, turmeric, black pepper, aniseed, star anis, cloves, anis, cinnamon, and slivered betel.*

Right*: A Malaysian dessert: sago pudding with palm sugar syrup and coconut milk. For generations of British, this dish was known simply as 'Gula Melaka' and no curry tiffin was complete without it.*

For weight-watchers, Malaysian fruits, such as mangosteen, are a delicious alternative.

A MOVEABLE FEAST

Far left: Campbell Street Municipal Market. Built by the British administration, circa 1900, on land that was part of the extensive acreage originally endowed to the Kapitan Keling Mosque. A bureaucratic concern for health and hygiene led to the mandatory construction of easily cleaned and maintained market buildings, throughout the British Empire. *Right*: Produce at Pulau Tikus Market. *Bottom row*: Green-leaf pyramids of nasi lemak. Fruits: durian, mangosteen and rambutan.

In an era when food shopping is all too often synonymous with pushing a trolley-load of plastic wrapped groceries through an anonymous supermarket, the Asian wet market is an exhilarating experience. The clamour, the colour, the smells - every walkway crammed with shoppers, stalls overflowing with fresh fish, meat, vegetables, herbs and even flowers, merchants shouting out their wares - this is life, first hand.

For the housewife of inner city George Town, an early morning walk to the Campbell Street or Chowrasta wet market forms part of the daily ritual. Armed with a strong wicker basket, she makes the rounds of her favourite stalls, prodding and haggling in true bazaar style. A quick pause for a bowl of *laksa* in the corner coffee shop, an impromptu chat with a friend and then back to the joyous fray.

These markets are more than just picturesque vending points: they fulfil the role of informal community centres and focal points of human exchange. Without them, George Town would be a poorer - and hungrier - place.

KEDAI KOPI : The Corner Coffee Shop

Bottom left: *Coffee shop, Cintra Street. The corner coffee shop or 'kedai kopi' is a familiar feature on most street corners of Malaysia. Open to the street, furnished with marble-topped tables and Bentwood chairs, for many people the coffee shop is an extension of both home and office. At all hours of the day clients can wander in, order delicious local coffee or a cooling drink, select a variety of dishes from the independently-run hawker stalls set up on the pavement outside and settle down for an hour or so of 'watching the world go by'.*

Top, near left: *The coconut house, Aboo Sittee Lane. The simple alternative to the coffee shop - coconut water sipped through a straw.*

Top, centre left: *The trishaw used to be George Town's favourite form of locomotion, taking children to school and housewives to the market. Nowadays, the trishaw has to rely on tourists for steady business - but for newcomers and residents alike, a ride through the old streets is always a thrill.*

Top, far left: *Pulau Tikus Market. Nasi lemak with a smile.*

Right: If you happen to be strolling down Beach Street of an afternoon you might meet Mr. Lee, who has managed to wedge Penang's smallest cake shop onto the back of his bicycle. Nyonya kuih - who could resist these sweet morsels, with their delicate flavours, interesting textures and gem-like colours and forms? These cakes can also be quite difficult to find and maybe this elusiveness makes them just that bit more enticing.

Penang housewives get up early and find them at the market, arranged in kaleidoscope patterns on big tin trays. The smiling ladies who sell the cakes are often the same ladies that have made them - this is very much a home industry.

Coconut milk, palm sugar, agar-agar and glutinous rice are just some of the locally produced ingredients used to make the kuih, whilst pandan leaves are used for colouring and to give that uniquely Malaysian flavour.

Far right: Tea time in George Town.

Left: The Esplanade makes a delightful waterfront setting for specialities such as pasembur, rojak and charcoal grilled satay served with a spicy peanut sauce.

Right: The informality and reasonable prices of hawker stall meals mean that Penangites tend to eat out often – and sometimes one meal just seems to run into the next!

Below: Kitchen theatre, Chulia Street. There's nothing like seeing a dish cooked before your very eyes.

STREET LIFE, NIGHT LIFE

As night begins to fall in George Town, its marvellous architecture becomes a backdrop for a most lively form of street life: the food hawkers and their busy flux of faithful clients and passers-by.

Penang's vibrant hawker tradition can be traced back to the settlement's fledgling days of the late 18th century. The large numbers of single male workers pouring into Penang from all parts of the globe were unable to cook in their makeshift accommodation and so, on each of those early street corners and alleyways, itinerant food vendors began to ply their wares, providing individual ethnic communities with a tasty, economic meal that conformed to their religious conventions.

Two hundred years later, Penang's tradition of excellent and varied hawker fare has become a major attraction for both local and overseas visitors. An evening spent flitting, butterfly style, from one hawker stall to the next, is a great way to really enter into the spirit of an island justifiably described as 'The Melting Pot of Asia'.

It makes sense to combine a gastronomic adventure at the hawker stalls in George Town or its environs with a late afternoon walk, soaking up the atmosphere, admiring the buildings and working up an appetite for the pleasures ahead.

Little by little, lights flicker on, the traffic is stilled and the city shifts into a different gear. Zinc tables and stools suddenly appear from thin air. Modest looking stalls open up to reveal a compact 'kitchen', complete with blackened woks and brightly coloured bowls and chopsticks.

Extended families, including wizened grandmothers and tiny, pyjama-clad children, crowd onto the sidewalks, ready for their evening meal, as sun-burnt tourists gaze, bemused, at the profusion of dishes, signposted in neon, that they have never heard of. *Lok lok, bak chang, hor fun…*

They settle for *char koay teow* - silky rice noodles, fried with prawns, eggs and bean sprouts - oyster omelette, hainanese chicken rice. To follow, crispy peanut pancakes and *chendol*, *pandan* flavoured noodles with coconut milk, brown sugar and shaved ice.

The crowds ebb and flow around the hawker stalls. Gas jets roar like fiery dragon's breath. The feast begins.

Above: Even the simplest roadside stall somehow manages to look aesthetically pleasing.
A neat stack of patterned and plain bowls, brightly coloured chopsticks or Chinese spoons - this attractive display is a far cry from the styrofoam offerings of the average fast food.
When it comes to hawker fare and coffee shops, locals have their personal favourites; they also know the particular time of day certain dishes are available. And festivals, of course, bring even more variety.

Batu Ferringhi

Tanjung Bungah

Teluk Bahang

Botanic
Gardens

Gurney Drive

Pulau
Tikus

Penang
Hill

George Town

Air Itam

Jelutong

Butterworth

Paya
Terubong

Balik
Pulau

Bayan
Baru

Pulau
Betong

Bayan
Lepas

Airport

Teluk
Kumbar

Gertak
Sanggul

PESIARAN GURNEY
(GURNEY DRIVE)

JALAN KELAWAI

JLN CLOVE HALL

JLN LARUT

.. ANSON

LRG ABOO SITTEE

JALAN RANGOON

LORONG SELAMAT

JALAN ZAIN

JALAN MACA

JALAN DA

GEORGE TOWN

SELECT BIBLIOGRAPHY

Queeny Chang. *Memories of a Nonya*. Eastern Universities Press.1981

Philip Davies. *Splendours of the Raj*. John Murray.1985.

Khoo Joo Ee. *The Straits Chinese*. The Pepin Press. 1996

The Encyclopedia of Malaysia: Architecture. Archipelago Press

Datuk Lim Chong Keat. *Penang Views*. Summer Times Publishing, 1986

Yeap Joo Kim. *The Patriarch*. Lee Teng Lay Pte. Ltd.1993

Lin Lee Loh-Lim. *The Blue Mansion*. L'Plan Sdn Bhd. 2002

James Low. *The British Settlement of Penang*. Oxford University Press. 1972. (1836).

Khoo Salma Nasution and Malcolm Wade. *Penang Postcards Collection, 1889-1930's*.
Areca Books, 2006 (2003).

Khoo Su Nin. *Streets of George Town: An Illustrated Guide To Penang's City Streets
 And Historic Attractions*. Penang: Janus Print & Resources, 2001 (1993).

The Penang Story. International Conference 2002. www.penangstory.net.my

Dilys Yap. *The Convent Light Street*. 2001

Graphic Design

Karen Bowen

Published by: **Areca Books**

120 Armenian Street, 10200 Penang, Malaysia

Tel:(604) 262 0123 Fax: (604) 263 3970

E-mail: areca@streamyx.com

Website: www.arecabooks.com

English edition, September 2006

French edition, September 2006

ISBN 983-42834-2-3

Printed by The Phoenix Press Sdn Bhd, Penang, Malaysia

Morgan the Musician in his Taxi.

ACKNOWLEDGEMENTS

Adlina Borhan

Cikgu Mohd Bahroodin Ahmad

Cecilia Mak Lai Ling

Eric Chang

Dato' Kee Phaik Cheen

Ahmad Chik

Logi Dhasan

Eric Fam Soo Seng

Louise Fontenoy

Danny and Molly Goon

Gwynn Jenkins

Pierre Lainé

Laurence Loh

Lin Lee Loh-Lim

Abdur-Razzaq Lubis

Yann Minois

Khoo Salma Nasution

Pamela Ong

Hugues de Melin

Joe Sidek

Peter Soon

Robert Tan

Teh Ewe Ooi

Lim Gaik Siang

Rebecca and David Wilkinson

Cikgu Mohamed Yahaya

Penang Heritage Trust

Alliance Française de Penang

Ruby at Mama's Restaurant

Sam's Batik House

Straits Furniture Arts & Antiques

And Morgan